ROUTLEDGE LIBRARY EDITIONS:
RETAILING AND DISTRIBUTION

THE DEVELOPMENT OF THE WHOLESALER IN THE UNITED STATES
1860–1900

THE DEVELOPMENT OF THE WHOLESALER IN THE UNITED STATES 1860–1900

BILL REID MOECKEL

Volume 2

Routledge
Taylor & Francis Group

LONDON AND NEW YORK

First published in 1986

This edition first published in 2013
by Routledge
2 Park Square, Milton Park, Abingdon, Oxon, OX14 4RN

Simultaneously published in the USA and Canada
by Routledge
711 Third Avenue, New York, NY 10017

Routledge is an imprint of the Taylor & Francis Group, an informa business

British Library Cataloguing in Publication Data
A catalogue record for this book is available from the British Library

ISBN: 978-0-415-51032-5 (Set)
eISBN: 978-0-203-10362-3 (Set)
ISBN: 978-0-415-62413-8 (Volume 2)
eISBN: 978-0-203-10370-8 (Volume 2)

Publisher's Note
The publisher has gone to great lengths to ensure the quality of this reprint but
points out that some imperfections in the original copies may be apparent.

Disclaimer
The publisher has made every effort to trace copyright holders and would
welcome correspondence from those they have been unable to trace.

Printed and bound by CPI Group (UK) Ltd, Croydon, CR0 4YY

AMERICAN
BUSINESS
HISTORY ★ A Garland Series
of Outstanding
Dissertations

Edited by
STUART BRUCHEY
Allan Nevins Professor of American
Economic History, Columbia University

THE DEVELOPMENT OF THE WHOLESALER
IN THE UNITED STATES
1860–1900

Bill Reid Moeckel

Garland Publishing, Inc.
New York & London ★ 1986

Library of Congress Cataloging-in-Publication Data

Moeckel, Bill Reid, 1925–
  The development of the wholesaler in the United
States, 1860–1900.

  Originally presented as the author's thesis (doctoral)
—University of Illinois at Urbana, 1953.
  Bibliography: p.
  1. Wholesale trade—United States—History—19th
century. I. Title.
HF5421.M64   1986   381'.2'0973   86-4760
ISBN 0-8240-8364-4

All volumes in this series are printed on acid-free,
250-year-life paper.

Printed in the United States of America

THE DEVELOPMENT OF THE WHOLESALER IN

THE UNITED STATES, 1860-1900

by

Bill Reid Moeckel

B.S., University of Illinois, 1948
M.S., University of Illinois, 1949

THESIS

Submitted in partial fulfillment of the requirements
for the degree of Doctor of Philosophy in Business
in the Graduate College of the
University of Illinois, 1953

Urbana, Illinois

TABLE OF CONTENTS

CHAPTER   PAGE

LIST OF TABLES   vi

LIST OF CHARTS   vi

I. INTRODUCTION   1

        Nature and scope of the study   2

        Definition of terms   3

        Institutional considerations   6

        Sources of data   8

        Organization of the study   8

II. WHOLESALERS AND WHOLESALE MARKETS IN 1860   11

        Volume of wholesale trade   11

        Wholesale market centers   13

            New York   14

            Boston   15

            Philadelphia   16

            Baltimore   17

            New Orleans   19

            Cincinnati   20

            Chicago   22

            St. Louis   25

            Louisville   26

CHAPTER   PAGE

        The wholesale merchant   28

                Specialization by the wholesaler   28

                Extension of credit   33

                Traveling salesmen   35

                Advertising   39

                Organization   40

                Shipping merchant, importer, exporter   41

        Agent middlemen in operation in 1860   43

                Auctioneers   43

                Commission merchants   45

                Brokers   47

                Commissions   48

        Summary   50

III.   GROWTH AND DEVELOPMENT OF WHOLESALE TRADING CENTERS,
        1860-1900   58

        Economic setting   58

        Changing relative importance of centers   64

        The two leading centers, New York and Chicago . .   65

                New York   65

                Chicago   68

        Other important coastal centers   75

                Philadelphia   76

                Boston and Baltimore   78

Other important interior centers   81

    Cincinnati   81

    Louisville   86

    St. Louis   90

Smaller cities as wholesale centers   94

    Kansas City   94

    Minneapolis and St. Paul   96

    Milwaukee   102

Summary   104

IV.   THE DEVELOPMENT OF THE WHOLESALE MERCHANT,
     1860–1900   112

Specialization by wholesale merchants   112

    Functional specialization   113

    Specialization by merchandise lines   115

Selling and sales promotion   117

    The development of traveling salesmen . . .   117

    Catalogs and printed price lists   129

The early development of wholesalers' brands . . .   132

Use of advertising by wholesale merchants   135

The wholesale merchant's credit operations   142

    Obtaining credit information   142

    Credit terms   147

    Financial assistance to retailers   150

CHAPTER   PAGE

      Physical facilities and organizations   152

          Facilities   152

          Organization   156

      Changing status of shipping merchants,
      importers and exporters   158

          Decline of the shipping merchant   158

          Reasons for the decline   158

      Importers and exporters   161

      Summary   164

  V.   AGENT WHOLESALERS   172

      Auctions   173

          Declining importance of auctions   173

          Volume of auction sales   176

          Reasons for the decline   179

      Commission merchants   182

          Commission merchants defined   182

          Declining in relative importance   183

          Handling large volumes in some lines   185

          Specialization by commission merchants   186

          Reasons for declining importance   189

      Selling agents   191

      Merchandise brokers   195

          Brokers defined   195

          Importance of brokers   196

CHAPTER   PAGE

      Manufacturers' agents   201

      Summary   203

VI. PARTICULAR COMPETITIVE PROBLEMS ENCOUNTERED
     BY THE WHOLESALER   210

      Major competitors of the wholesaler   210

      Efforts to eliminate the wholesaler   212

          Manufacturers selling direct   212

          Retailers buying direct   217

          Farmers' efforts to eliminate middlemen . . .   221

      Competitive efforts and tools employed by
      the wholesaler   222

          Formation of associations   223

          Private brands   226

          Factor or rebate plan   228

      Summary   231

VII. SUMMARY AND CONCLUSIONS   237

BIBLIOGRAPHY   249

LIST OF TABLES

TABLE   PAGE

I   Number of Establishments, Volume of Sales, Annual Payrolls and Number of Employees by Types of Wholesaling Operations, 1948   4

II   Estimates of the Total Value of Goods Sold at Wholesale in the United States by Sources and Decades, 1850-1900   12

III   Business Fluctuations in the United States, 1860-1900   63

IV   Volume of Business Transacted in Leading Commercial Cities by Wholesale and Retail Dealers in Merchandise and by Auctioneers and Merchandise Brokers, Fiscal Year Ending June 30, 1867   69

V   Volume of Sales at Wholesale in Four Leading Lines of Trade, Cincinnati, 1860-1900   87

VI   Volume of Sales at Wholesale in Selected Lines of Trade in St. Louis for 1890 and 1900 . . .   93

VII   Wholesale Trade of Kansas City for the Year Ending June 30, 1891   97-98

VIII   Volume of Sales at Wholesale by Lines of Trade, Minneapolis, 1891-92   103

IX   Value of Merchandise Imports and Exports, United States, 1860-1900   162

LIST OF CHARTS

I   Index of Wholesale Prices, 1860-1900   62

CHAPTER I

INTRODUCTION

Although the scientific study of marketing is relatively new, certain aspects of it have been analyzed in considerable detail. A large body of literature exists, for example, on the various phases of retailing and advertising. Studies of the growth and development of the institutions important in these areas are available. It is only in the past decade or two, however, that much attention has been given to the study of wholesalers and wholesaling. Consequently, there is a scarcity of literature in the general field of wholesaling and most of what there is concerns itself only with the present.[1]

Perhaps this lack of attention to wholesaling and its institutional factors and forces can be explained on the basis of the general feeling that has prevailed from time to time that the wholesaler should be eliminated. It may be due to the lack of pertinent and readily available data, to a failure to recognize the importance of the problem, to the small size of wholesale establishments, or to the reticence of wholesalers in the past to divulge information on their operations. Whatever the reasons for the inadequate attention to the general area of wholesaling it is apparent that here is a fertile field for scientific investigation by students of marketing.

That wholesalers and wholesaling occupy an important place in our economy is attested to by the facts set down in Table I. About 2,500,000 persons are engaged in wholesaling, approximately sixty-five percent of whom are employed in merchant wholesaler operations. Total wholesale sales in 1948 were over 188 billions of dollars, or about seventy percent as large as the gross national product of 259 billions. Of a national income in the same year of 223 billion dollars, about 13 billions, or six percent, arose from wholesale trade; this latter figure represents the value added by wholesaling.[2]

Nature and Scope of the Study

The nature of this study is historical. It is based on a belief in the fundamental importance of a knowledge of the past as a foundation upon which to build a fuller understanding of the present so as to be able better to prepare for the future.

The purposes of the study are:

1. To trace and analyze the development of the wholesaler in the United States between 1860 and 1900.

2. To set the analysis against the general economic background and the economic occurrences which had the greatest influence upon changes in the wholesaler's organization and operations.

3. To show the manner in which the wholesaler adapted himself to the changing economic environment.

Such an analysis, set in its proper frame of reference, is
necessarily broad even though the period of time under consideration
is restricted. The particular period for the study, 1860 to 1900,
was selected because it was not until about 1860 that wholesaling
and retailing were definitely separated on a broad scale as two
distinct types of marketing operations. Developments before 1860
were but a prelude to the era of important innovations and rapid
growth by the wholesaler in the last forty years of the nineteenth
century. At best any dating of this nature is arbitrary but 1900
marks roughly the end of an era. After that time new and
significant developments took place in wholesaling and among
wholesalers which merit discussion in a separate study. The advent
of the limited-function wholesaler, the rise of chains, use of the
automobile, and so on were all factors affecting the changes after
1900.

As previously noted there are studies available for the
preceding and subsequent periods but there are none, as such, for
the period under consideration. It is hoped, therefore, that this
work may help to fill a gap in the literature and to provide a basis
for further investigation.

Definition of Terms

Since loose definitions and careless terminology characterize
much of the literature examined, it seems expedient to pause here

TABLE I

NUMBER OF ESTABLISHMENTS, VOLUME OF SALES, ANNUAL PAYROLLS AND
NUMBER OF EMPLOYEES BY TYPES OF WHOLESALING OPERATIONS, 1948

Type	Establishments	Sales (000's omitted)	Payrolls (000's omitted)	Employees
Total All Operations	243,366	$188,688,801	$7,990,713	2,546,279
Merchant Wholesalers	146,518	79,766,589	5,064,381	1,614,813
Manufacturer's Sales Branches and Offices	23,768	52,738,577	1,921,654	502,396
Petroleum Bulk Stations and Terminals	29,451	10,615,650	345,847	136,418
Agents and Brokers	24,361	34,610,092	350,148	123,470
Assemblers of Farm Products	19,268	10,957,893	308,683	169,182

*Includes proprietors
 Source: United States Census of Business: 1948, Vol. IV

and define the basic terms used in the study. Other terms will be defined as the need arises.

<u>Wholesaling</u> includes all the operations of middlemen and producers in getting processed goods from their point of production to retailers or processors, and in getting raw materials from their point of production to processors.[3]

Middlemen are of two types, <u>merchant middlemen</u> who take title to the goods they handle, and <u>agent middlemen</u> who negotiate purchases and/or sales but do not take title.

The <u>wholesale merchant</u> is a merchant middleman who sells, usually in fairly large quantities, to retailers and other merchants and/or to industrial, institutional, and commercial users but who does not sell in significant amounts to ultimate consumers.

The term <u>jobber</u> is currently considered synonymous with merchant wholesaler and will be so considered here unless a special usage is indicated in the text. In 1860 jobbers were defined as merchants who purchased goods from importers and resold them in smaller lots to retailers.

A <u>commission merchant</u>, or <u>factor</u>, is an agent wholesaler transacting business in his own name who has possession of, but not title to, the goods.

A <u>broker</u> is an agent wholesaler who buys or sells for his principal without having title to, or physical control of, the goods.

Institutional Considerations

The Census divides wholesale trade into five major categories:[4]

1. Merchant wholesalers

2. Sales branches and sales offices maintained by
    manufacturing or mining enterprises apart from their
    producing plants

3. Agents, merchandise or commodity brokers, and commission
    merchants

4. Petroleum bulk stations

5. Assemblers of farm products

To attempt to examine the development of all the middlemen
engaged in wholesale trade would be a Herculean task and would
result in a very superficial examination of any one. Therefore, it
is felt that an analysis of the rise of selected middlemen engaged
in wholesale trade will be both more valuable and practicable. For
this purpose categories one and three of the census classification
have been chosen, merchant wholesalers and agents and brokers.
Within these classifications particular reference will be made to
what are sometimes termed the traditional jobbing lines, that is,
groceries, hardware, drugs, and dry goods, from which to draw
exemplary and expository material. The remaining types of middlemen
will be considered where their operations and activities have a
direct bearing on the adjustments to change, and the policies and
methods adopted by the merchant wholesalers, agents, and brokers.

The early importance and rapid development of merchant
wholesalers and agents and brokers was the primary basis upon which

the necessary decisions were made in laying out the scope of this study. Furthermore, as evidence of their continuing importance, it is interesting to note that these two groups of intermediaries accounted for about sixty percent or more than 114 billion dollars of the total wholesale trade of approximately 188 billions in 1948.[5] This in spite of the frequent predictions made in the past that the wholesaler had long since outlived his usefulness and would soon be displaced. Sales branches and offices of manufacturers receive only secondary consideration in this discussion, not because they were unimportant, but because they were not independent intermediaries in wholesale trade and although they engage in wholesaling operations are not, by definition, wholesalers. However, since such sales branches and offices were important in determining the competitive climate in which the wholesaler operated, and thus directly affected his development, they will be considered in the light of their impact on this development. Agents, merchandise brokers, and commission merchants or factors were of considerable importance during the period under discussion and, therefore, deserve primary attention. Little attention is given to assemblers and bulk tank stations because the latter were of little importance during the period and the former are primarily concerned with farm products and deserve more attention in a study devoted to the evolution of marketing in that area.

Sources of Data

The sources of data for a study of this nature are as widely scattered as they are numerous. Although it was not until 1929 that the first Census of Distribution was taken, there is a limited amount of pertinent data available in connection with the various censuses of manufactures; for example, in 1840 information on commerce was gathered in connection with the census of that year. A second important government source is the reports on Internal Trade of the United States by the Bureau of Statistics of the Treasury Department. The early commercial magazines and trade directories also furnish some quantitative data as well as much other valuable information. The annual proceedings of the associations of wholesalers and reports of Boards of Trade and Chambers of Commerce are further examples of valuable sources relevant to this period.

Autobiographies, biographies, memoirs and reminiscences of men prominent in the field provide much of value and interest in analyzing the development of the wholesaler. Books dealing with economic and industrial history, city and area histories, and general histories of commerce, all provide data bearing on the setting of the problem and also contain directly related bits of information useful in the study.

Organization of the Study

Chapter II includes a statement and analysis of the situation in 1860 with reference to the general economic picture and the position of the wholesalers and markets important at the time. Certain basic trends in the wholesaler's mode of operation stand out during the last half of the nineteenth century; for example, the tendency toward specialization in method of operation and type of merchandise lines handled. The purpose of Chapter II is to clarify these trends and point out the business and economic occurrences from which they arose.

The remaining chapters trace these various threads of development, or trends, to 1900. Chapter III is an examination of the evolution of the various wholesale market centers during this period, the reasons for their growth and importance, and their effect on the wholesaler and his operations. The fourth chapter concerns itself with an analysis of the changes in functions, policies, and methods of organization and operation of the wholesale merchant. Chapter V analyzes the changing status and practices of agent wholesalers after 1860. The trends toward development of new types of operations and increasing specialization are especially noticeable here. The sixth chapter is a consideration of the particular competitive problems encountered by the wholesaler and the steps he took in meeting them. Finally, the major findings and conclusions of the study are presented in Chapter VII.

FOOTNOTES – CHAPTER I

[1]Notable among the few exceptions to this statement are: Fred M. Jones, "Middlemen in the Domestic Trade of the United States, 1800-1860," Illinois Studies in the Social Sciences, Volume 21:3 (May, 1937); and "Grocery Wholesaling in Illinois from 1900-1929," Bulletin No. 36, Bureau of Business Research, University of Illinois, 1931.

[2]United States Census of Business, 1948.

[3]Paul D. Converse, Harvey W. Huegy, and Robert V. Mitchell, The Elements of Marketing (New York: Prentice-Hall, Inc., 1952), p. 304.

[4]Wholesale trade is a narrower term than wholesaling. The former includes only those operations indicated. Wholesaling, on the other hand, includes sales made by manufacturers and mines from their home offices and sales made by farmers and others not operating from wholesale establishments.

[5]See Table I.

CHAPTER II

WHOLESALERS AND WHOLESALE MARKETS IN 1860

Volume of Wholesale Trade

The total volume of wholesale trade in the United States in 1860 cannot be determined precisely. Some indication of its magnitude, however, can be derived from estimates of the value of domestic trade for that year. One source places the total at $3,500,000,000.[1] Another suggests $4,800,000,000 as a reasonable amount.[2] These figures are based on the aggregate value of manufactures, agricultural products, minerals, and imports and measure the value of internal commerce in terms of a single transaction in those items. Careful interpretation and application of these data provide a good measure of the magnitude of wholesaling in 1860. It is also possible to make similar estimates for the rest of the period as has been done in Table II.

In order to arrive at a closer approximation of the amount of internal trade, the value of merchandise exported and re-exported should be deducted from the preceding estimates. If the $333,600,000 of merchandise exports and re-exports in 1860 are deducted from the first estimate above, the figure becomes $3,166,000,000 which approximates the estimate given in Table II. The remainder of the difference is probably largely accounted for on the basis of differences in technique. The last column in the table

TABLE II

ESTIMATES OF THE TOTAL VALUE OF GOODS SOLD AT WHOLESALE
IN THE UNITED STATES BY SOURCES AND DECADES, 1850-1900
(Millions of dollars)[a]

Year	Agriculture[b]	Manufacturing[c]	Mining[b]	Fishing[b]	Imports of Merchandise[d]	Total in Millions	Less Value of Merchandise Exports and Re-exports[d]	Total Value of Goods Sold at Wholesale[e]
1850	$ 764.9	$ 1,019.1	$ 23.0	$10.0	$173.5	$ 1,990.5	$ 144.3	$ 1,846.2
1860	1,088.2	1,885.9	62.0	12.9	353.6	3,402.6	333.6	3,069.0
1870	1,783.2	3,385.9	145.0	15.0	435.9	5,765.0	392.8	5,372.2
1880	1,476.0	5,369.6	218.0	33.8	667.9	7,765.3	835.6	6,929.2
1890	2,260.0	9,372.4	329.0	38.2	789.3	12,788.9	857.8	11,931.1
1900	3,688.0	13,000.1	591.0	42.5	849.9	18,171.4	1,394.5	16,776.9

[a]In producer's current dollars, point of production.
[b]King, Wilford I., The Wealth and Income of the People of the United States (New York, 1915), p. 138.
[c]U.S. Bureau of the Census, Census of Manufactures.
[d]Department of Commerce, Bureau of Foreign and Domestic Commerce.
[e]See p. 13 for comments on this column.

is a representation of the value of goods sold at wholesale in the various years.

A further refinement, but one for which data are not available, would be to deduct the value of goods consumed by their producers and the amount sold directly to consumers by producers. To secure the figures for wholesaling, however, it is not necessary to adjust for the amount of goods sold directly since the wholesaling functions are not eliminated in such operations but only combined with manufacturing and retailing. The values in the last column of Table II do not represent wholesalers' sales but the total volume of wholesale business as defined in Chapter I. These data represent the values of the goods at the point of production in producer's current dollars.

Considering that some of the raw materials passed through several hands on the way to the manufacturer and that his products were subsequently handled by one or a succession of several middlemen, it is apparent that the total volume of transactions at wholesale was much larger than indicated by the figures in the table.[3]

Wholesale Market Centers

The internal commerce in 1860 flowed in certain well-defined currents between the major wholesale centers. Of these there were eight with a population of over one hundred thousand. In the East, New York, Boston, Philadelphia, and Baltimore competed for the

markets of the South and West. The magnitude of this trade is
indicated by an estimate that, just prior to the Civil War, New
England alone marketed in the South over sixty million dollars worth
of manufactured goods, fish, molasses, and the like and purchased
over fifty-five millions in cotton, flour, and similar items.[4] That
the coastal trade between the northern and southern ports was large
is shown by the fact that shipments of over $100,000,000 worth of
boots and shoes and other manufactures were made to the South
annually from northern ports.[5] Baltimore and Philadelphia merchants
struggled for the interior trade. Cincinnati was one of the
earliest of the western wholesale centers to develop and by 1860 was
attempting to lure the trade of the interior merchants away from New
York and other Eastern centers. Cincinnati, Chicago, and St. Louis
dominated the wholesale trade of the West in 1860 and were competing
vigorously among themselves, as well as with the more distant
centers in the East, for the western and southern trade. In the
South New Orleans handled the traffic in manufactured goods coming
down the rivers from Cincinnati and Pittsburgh and dealt in
agricultural products from the St. Louis area. This river traffic
was at an all-time high in 1860.[6]

New York. The competition between New York and Philadelphia
was especially keen with the former playing the dominant role. A
Philadelphia author conceded in 1859 that "...the City [New York]
has culminated into the Metropolis of America, whose commercial sway

seems to be as far beyond the reach of competition, as her enterprise has yet been beyond successful imitation."[7] In 1859 it was estimated that New York firms sold to the southern cotton states alone goods valued at $131,000,000 and that it was probable that these five states provided a total volume of business for New York of about $200,000,000 annually.[8] Furthermore, the same source places the value of trade between New York and eight of its neighboring states, including Pennsylvania, at six hundred millions of dollars.[9]

Boston. The dominant center of wholesale trade in 1860, then, was New York although there were some lines of goods in which other cities were superior. In the boot and shoe trade, for example, Boston with two hundred wholesale houses surpassed New York with only 56, in both number of firms and sales.[10] Annual shipments in this trade from Boston to all parts of the southern and western United States reached 37,500,000 pairs with an aggregate value of $43,000,000 in 1859.[11] During that year there was a "more general concentration of the Shoe Trade in Boston: Manufacturers from all parts of New England have been flocking here opening offices and stores for the display and sale of goods."[12] Boston was also prominent in other lines of wholesale trade. It supplied considerable amounts of clothing to merchants in the West and Northwest and was second only to New York in the wholesale grocery trade.[13] Although the wholesale hardware trade was centered in New

York there were in Boston in 1859 some seventy wholesale hardware merchants with an annual sales volume of about eight million dollars.[14]

Philadelphia. The importance of Philadelphia as a wholesale center is indicated by the magnitude of its wholesale dry goods trade which alone amounted to $75,000,000 in 1860 plus an additional $25,000,000 for partially manufactured dry goods.[15] This large trade was not considered an unmixed blessing because Philadelphia was losing some trade to New York which it felt should be retained for the benefit of its own merchants:

> Indeed, there is no class of domestic fabrics which does not send a large quantity of goods annually direct from the factories to New York for sale, and the evil is one well worth the attention of our merchants and bankers. It is out of the power of manufacturers to control this course of business, but quite within the power of commission and distributing merchants, aided by proper banking faculties, to do so.[16]

This report was not the only one that emphasized the importance of the concentration of banking facilities and capital in New York as the basis for that city's preeminence in trade. This, of course, was not the only, or the most important, reason.[17] New York was the leading port for exports and imports because of superior location and the facilities connecting her with a rich interior area. This region furnished quantities of goods for export and provided a broad market for imports, all of which formed a strong base upon which New York built a dominant position in both foreign and domestic trade.

Baltimore. The fourth of the major eastern centers at this time was Baltimore. The following data taken from the annual report of trade by the Baltimore American give a conservative and reasonably accurate representation of the leading lines of trade and their relative importance in that city:[18]

Boots and Shoes......$ 3,650,000	Iron...................$ 2,000,000
Books and Papers..... 3,000,000	Leather............... 3,905,000
Coal................. 3,100,000	Live Stock............ 3,804,000
Ready-made Clothing.. 7,000,000	Lumber................ 1,675,000
Copper............... 2,500,000	Molasses.............. 1,000,000
Cotton............... 2,600,000	Naval Stores.......... 267,000
Coffee............... 4,000,000	Oysters............... 4,500,000
Drugs, Paints, etc... 1,500,000	Provisions............ 7,000,000
Dry Goods............ 30,000,000	Piano Trade........... 375,000
Earthenware.......... 1,250,000	Salt.................. 100,000
Foreign Fruits....... 1,500,000	Sugar................. 7,000,000
Salted Fish.......... 325,000	Leaf Tobacco.......... 2,775,000
Flour................ 5,000,000	Manufactured Tobacco.. 4,100,000
Grain................ 7,087,000	Cigars................ 800,000
Guano................ 3,000,000	Vessels Built......... 200,000
Hardware............. 4,000,000	Wool.................. 400,000
Foreign Spirits...... 1,500,000	Teas.................. 300,000
Whisky............... 1,500,000	Soap and Candles...... 740,000
Hat Trade............ 750,000	Preserved Fruits...... 215,000

Total...$124,418,800

The same souce suggests that if the unenumerated items were added the total of trade would have reached $154,000,000 which is very close to the estimate of $150,000,000 given in the annual report of the Prices Current.[19]

Baltimore and Philadelphia were especially active in competing with one another for the trade of the territory to the west. The

latter was more successful in this bitter rivalry, so, by 1860
Baltimore was centering its efforts to develop new sources of trade
primarily on the South and Southwest. That these efforts were not
too successful is indicated by the following account in which an
attempt is made to attract trade by appealing to political as well
as economic motives:

> We have been reading and hearing, for some
> years, that it was the desire and intention of
> Southern merchants to withdraw their patronage
> from the abolition cities of the North, to those
> having a common interest in the maintenance of
> the peculiar institution. As yet, we do not see
> that this principle has been carried out to any
> marked extent....The claims which Baltimore
> has always urged and sustained, wholly
> independent of such considerations, should
> secure her, we think, a larger share of Southern
> trade than she now commands; and if there be any
> practical meaning in these declarations, the
> results must soon be plainly manifest in a
> largely increased business with that section of
> our country. For liquors, for domestic dry
> goods, for provisions, for manufactured tobacco,
> for groceries, flour, and other almost equally
> indispensable articles to the Southern merchant
> and planter, there is no market north of
> Baltimore--and we challenge a contradiction of
> these facts--that can offer greater advantages
> or better terms to purchasers. We call upon
> Southern merchants, therefore, if they mean what
> they say, to test the truth of our assertions.[20]

A lack of any real degree of success in this effort was
inevitable. Not only was New Orleans dominant as a southern market
center but the interior cities such as St. Louis and Louisville were
attempting to expand their trade areas southward.

New Orleans. One of the early wholesale trading centers of the country was New Orleans. The two decades preceding the Civil War were particularly prosperous ones for this market. The value of produce received at New Orleans from the interior increased from $49,822,115 in 1840 to $185,211,254 in 1860. During this period New Orleans had regular steamboat lines to all the important river towns, Pittsburgh, Cincinnati, Louisville, and St. Louis and dominated the trade carried on the Tennessee, Cumberland, Red, Yazoo and other rivers.[21] New Orleans, St. Louis, and Cincinnati were competing vigorously for domination of the river traffic but New Orleans was unsurpassed in this trade before 1860. Over two million tons of freight reached the city by river that season and the total trade in the receipt and shipment of produce, and in exports and imports, amounted to more than $473,000,000.[22] In that year the receipts of produce from the interior at New Orleans reached a peak but were abruptly shut off by the War the following year and New Orleans never again attained its former relative position of importance.

The decline of New Orleans as the dominant center of trade in the Mississippi Valley was inevitable; the war only hastened it. Well before 1860 forces were gathering which were undermining the foundations of this commerce and causing the city's trade area to contract steadily. The development of the Erie canal and Great Lakes waterways, the rapid expansion of the railroad net, and the early lack of good rail facilities serving New Orleans account

largely for the inroads of competing centers on New Orleans' trade
area. Eastern wholesalers were able to deal directly with interior
merchants rather than having their trade routed through that city, a
more circuitous and expensive route. Factors, other than the
diversion of trade from New Orleans due to canal and railroad
construction, contributing to the relative decline were: 1. the
absence of manufacturing; 2. poor storage and marketing facilities
for products other than cotton; 3. high port charges and river and
harbor obstructions.

These, then, are some indications of the nature and importance
of the major wholesale centers in the East and South which developed
early and had grown to sizable proportions in terms of the total of
domestic trade in 1860. The largest of the centers, New York,
Philadelphia, and Boston were competing vigorously, at times it
would seem even viciously, and in addition their positions were
being assailed by the rapidly growing and progressive centers in the
West.

Cincinnati. Among the first of the interior wholesale centers
to challenge the domination of the Eastern cities was Cincinnati.
The most extensive wholesale business was carried on by the dry
goods and grocery houses although drug, boot and shoe, hardware, and
imported and fancy goods dealers did a considerable volume of
business with country merchants in Ohio, Indiana, Illinois, and
Kentucky.[23] According to the Cincinnati Directory for 1860 there

were in the city at that time 97 wholesale grocers, 55 wholesale dry goods houses, 70 wholesale clothiers, and 9 wholesale merchants in the drug trade, along with numerous other middlemen operating as brokers, auctioneers, and commission and produce and forwarding merchants. The value of goods of all kinds sold to the country merchants was estimated at $100,000,000 in 1859.[24] The challenge to the eastern wholesale markets and the lure to the western trade were based on a number of advantages claimed for the Cincinnati market. They were outlined by a contemporary in 1859 as follows:

> 1. The merchant who goes east is compelled, in order advantageously to make up his full assortment, to visit Boston, New York, Philadelphia, and Baltimore. This is attended with traveling and hotel expenses, as well as loss of time at home of still greater value, which puts at least five percent on his season's purchases.

> 2. By purchasing in Cincinnati, at a distance so short and a point of such easy access from home, the western merchant is enabled to buy in three or four days what will require as many weeks in a trip east. This is not merely a saving of time, but a means of choosing the period of absence, not allowable in long and distant journeys. Almost any man can arrange and provide for an absence from home of a few days, but every merchant's business is sure to suffer in the absence of as many weeks.

> 3. He could obviate the risk of accumulating unsalable goods; keeping his supplies within the limits of his sales by making smaller and more frequent purchases.

> 4. In making bills oftener, he has a greater average of credit, as well as greater convenience in the division of payments.[25]

This does not mean, however, that Cincinnati wholesale merchants were sitting passively waiting for business to come to their door. They were energetically seeking out customers and attempting to broaden their markets. A number of the houses in the wholesale clothing business, for example, had branches at "Louisville, Chicago, St. Louis, all the important towns on the Missouri and Mississippi Rivers, and at various places in this state, Kentucky, and Tennessee, so that the trade, in this way, is largely extended; and as prices at those branch houses are the same as here, adding freight, local competition is out of the question."[26] Although this is not the earliest instance of branch house wholesaling it is one of the first and is indicative of the aggressiveness of Cincinnati wholesalers in their efforts to secure business. These efforts resulted in a widening trade area and furthered localization of industry in the rapidly developing marketing center which, in turn, further stimulated trade and commerce and enhanced Cincinnati's position as a leading wholesale center in 1860.

Chicago. By 1850 Chicago was a prominent wholesale market and grew to such an extent in the next 10 years that it was seriously challenging the position of St. Louis and Cincinnati as the dominant centers of the western trade. The following figures show the volume of the business done in certain lines in Chicago in 1860 and are indicative of the general magnitude of wholesale trade:[27]

Dry Goods.....................................	$15,000,000
Groceries.....................................	8,200,000
Iron and Hardware.............................	3,650,000
Boots and shoes, Clothing, and other..........	5,000,000
Total.................................	$31,850,000

The dry goods trade was the most important and it drew country
merchants from a widely extended area throughout the West and
Northwest. The Panic of 1857 gave particular impetus to the growth
of Chicago's wholesale dry goods trade and enhanced the city's
position with regard to the competition of Eastern centers in this
line. The country merchants, in many cases, were caught with large
stocks and suffered considerable losses due to inventory
devaluation following the Panic. The Chicago wholesale merchants
had weathered the financial storm reasonably well and so were in a
better position, both financially and geographically, to sell the
smaller centers further west on credit and in smaller quantities,
than were wholesalers in some of the other centers. This situation
was underlined by an editorial in a leading Chicago newspaper urging
western merchants to come to Chicago and buy cautiously and avoid
overstocking during the 1860 spring buying. It is better to order
twice, it editorialized, than to get a lot of unsalable goods on the
shelves and:

> This advice is the more needful as western
> firms are now in much better credit than they
> were a year ago...those who have paid promptly
> during the fearful revulsion through which we
> have passed, are good for all they can be
> induced to buy.[28]

That the country merchants were quick to take advantage of the credit being offered by Chicago houses, and also of the proximity of the market to order more frequently and thus avoid overstocking, is shown by the rapid growth of the wholesale dry goods trade in that city. The aggregate sales of these wholesale merchants in 1859 were nearly twenty-four percent greater than in 1858 and by 1864 Chicago had become the dry goods center of the country outside of New York.[29] There is some doubt as to the exact number of dry goods firms handling this business in Chicago in 1860, a conservative source placing it at six.[30] Expansion in all the departments of wholesale trade was taking place before the Civil War.

From 1857 to 1861 the development of the grocery trade was steady and houses were continually enlarging their sales territories.[31] The wholesale clothing trade grew from practically nothing in 1850 to an annual volume of $2,000,000 in 1860 with several firms competing for the trade. The boot and shoe trade, which had first been established in Chicago in 1851, grew rapidly until by 1859 there were 11 houses engaged in wholesaling boots and shoes, not including firms who also conducted retail operations.[32] These firms shipped merchandise to points throughout Michigan, Northern Indiana, Illinois, Iowa, Wisconsin, and Minnesota and a few goods were marketed in Northern Missouri.[33] This provides an idea of the extensive trade area served by Chicago wholesalers. It is interesting to note that in 1860 the total value of manufactures produced in Chicago was about $13,500,000 while the dry goods trade alone amounted to $15,000,000, and wholesale sales in four lines totaled more than $31,000,000 or over twice as much as the aggregate value of manufactured goods.

St. Louis. Although it would seem, from the writings of business men and citizens, that Chicagoans regarded St. Louis in 1860 as a practically defunct rival in the triangle of competition which included Cincinnati as the eastern corner, this was not so.[34] By that time, it is true, the rate of growth of St. Louis had been decelerated but still it occupied a significant place in the wholesale structure in internal trade. As early as 1854 the wholesalers in various branches of trade extended sales into all parts of the West from Minnesota to Texas.[35] By 1860 St. Louis was undisputedly the commercial capital of Missouri and dominated much of the trade in adjoining states and territories. It surpassed in its trade every other place on the river north of New Orleans. It is estimated that at its peak the steamboat trade approximated two hundred millions of dollars per year.[36] The Mississippi and Illinois to the North, the Ohio and its tributaries to the East, and the Missouri to the West furnished access to a rich territory from which to draw produce to be shipped South to New Orleans and in which to market goods imported from the East and abroad as well as St. Louis' own manufactures.

To handle this trade entering and emanating from St. Louis, a large number of wholesale houses had been established by 1880. By that time there were 52 wholesale grocery firms with a total volume

of over $22,000,000.[37] Illustrative of the rapidity with which St.

Louis developed up to the Civil War was a report by six dry goods

firms whose statements showed sales in 1845 of $1,119,657 and whose

sales in 1853 were $4,074,782. The total dry goods trade in the

latter year probably aggregated more than $12,000,000 since there

were at that time over 20 dry goods houses in the city.[38]

Louisville. By 1860 Louisville had developed into an important

wholesale center. Largely holding its own competitively with St.

Louis, it was making serious inroads on the Southern commerce which

Cincinnati had dominated and considered its own since almost the

turn of the century when Chicago and St. Louis were non-existent and

Louisville was little more than a clearing in the wilderness.

Early railroad construction was largely tributary to natural

waterways and offered little competition to river trade. But with

the opening of the Louisville and Nashville Railroad in 1859

Louisville was given access by rail via Nashville to the markets in

Knoxville, Chattanooga, Memphis and Charleston, and many other

important points throughout the South. The slower and less

dependable river transport was not able to compete and there was a

steady deflection of traffic from river to railroad, that is, from

Cincinnati to Louisville.[39] This changing current of trade was as

calamitous for Cincinnati as it was beneficial to Louisville because

the former had enjoyed a particularly lucrative commerce with the

South and because the extension of railroads from the coast to the
Mississippi Valley in the 1850's had brought new competitors for
Cincinnati in the North.

Reliable statistics are not available on the number of
wholesalers and their volume of sales in Louisville for 1860. There
are, however, data available for 1852 and from these can be inferred
the probable structure of wholesale trade for 1860, bearing in mind
the great impetus given this business in 1859 by the opening of the
Louisville and Nashville Railroad. The dry goods trade included 25
firms with an annual total volume of $5,853,000. The grocery trade
was about twice as large with 39 houses whose sales aggregated
$10,623,000. There were numerous other wholesalers in boots and
shoes, drugs, hardware, and hats who brought the total of wholesale
firms in Louisville to 103 with a volume of $20,321,000.[40] This
figure, it should be noted, does not include the sales made by
middlemen other than merchant wholesalers such as agents and
brokers. The number of wholesale houses in 1857 was placed at
eighty-five.[41] This would indicate a decrease of 18 firms in five
years which seems improbable, although there were undoubtedly some
failures as a result of the Panic of 1857.

The seeming inconsistency in the numbers is probably due
largely to differences in the basis of classification of the
business houses involved. The same source states that in 1867 there
were 287 wholesale businesses in operation which would bear out the

conclusion above of very rapid growth of the Louisville wholesale market after 1859. On the basis of the preceding it would seem reasonable to place the number of wholesale firms in Louisville in 1860 at 145. This is a conservative estimate since it assumes a constant rate of growth between 1857 and 1867 while, in all probability, the rate was considerably greater preceding the Civil War, during and immediately following which, southern trade especially was depressed.

The Wholesale Merchant

Specialization by the wholesaler. Such was the situation as it existed in 1860 with respect to wholesale markets and centers of trade. Chief among the middlemen operating in these markets was the merchant wholesaler. Many of these merchants were selling strictly at wholesale but more of them were combining other operations with their merchant wholesaling. Some advertised themselves as wholesalers, as wholesalers and commmission merchants, and numerous ones operated at both the wholesale and retail level, selling to consumers as well as retailers. Many of the wholesale-retail combinations were wholesale merchants who added so-called retail departments in order to fill in the slack season between the spring and fall peaks in wholesale sales. This class would fall under the heading of semi-jobbers in current terminology.

The semi-annual fluctuations in the wholesale merchant's sales were due to the practice, still common in 1860, of the country merchants making major buying trips to the wholesale centers, once in the spring and again in the fall, buying enough at one time to supply their customers during the intervening periods. That this practice had not always been the case is indicated in an account in 1860 of the domestic boot and shoe trade, one of the largest in the country:

> About the year 1829 the wholesale houses in Boston introduced a new system of business, which has rendered that city the great emporium of the trade in New England. Previously it had been the custom for dealers to consign their goods, on their own account, to merchants in the principal cities of the United States and the West Indies. This was found to be unprofitable when competition had grown strong, and lead to the failure of many of the large houses. During the last thirty years or more, it has been customary for the large manufacturers and jobbers to sell their goods at their places of business, thus compelling the market to come to their doors instead of seeking it themselves. The financial embarrassments of 1857-8 severely tested the vigor of this branch of trade which was found to withstand the shock equal to any in the country.[42]

The success of this policy can probably be attributed largely to the existence of a sellers' market up to about 1860. The gradual shift to a buyers' market after the Civil War would account for the displacement of this method of sale by the more aggressive selling methods which characterized the latter part of the century. There were other factors, of course, which were also important in accounting for the semi-annual peaks, including the difficulties of transportation and communication combined with the fact that the markets were very scattered. The conclusion might be drawn then, using the boot and shoe trade as an example, that to overcome the evils of consignment selling the wholesale merchants and manufacturers selling at wholesale forced the market to come to them, possible because a sellers' market prevailed. This led to the seasonal peaks in volume already mentioned.

In an effort to level off their annual sales curves the wholesale merchants established retail departments to bolster business during the slack periods, which explains the existence of many retail departments. It is also true that some of these merchants started as retailers and, as the markets widened with improvements in transportation, they saw opportunities for increased profit by acting in a wholesale as well as a retail capacity, hence the dual operation. These factors account, in part at least, for the prevalence of the combined wholesale-retail, or semi-jobber, type of operation in 1860.

That the degree of specialization depends upon the extent of the market is borne out in examining the wholesale structure throughout the latter half of the nineteenth century. As the markets were continually widened, with the establishment of better means of transportation and increased industrialization, the wholesale merchant tended to specialize more and more and to concentrate on wholesale operations as distinct from retailing. That is not to say that there was no integration later because there was, but by 1860 the beginnings, at least, of a trend toward the exclusively wholesale type of operation, as separate from some combination, were discernible.

The trend toward specialization by merchandise lines was also well-established by this time and continued with the expansion of the markets. In 1860 there were wholesale merchants, selling at wholesale only, who specialized in the following lines:[43]

Boots and Shoes	Hats and Caps
China, Crockery, Glassware	Hosiery and Gloves
Clothing	Laces and Embroideries
Coal	Millinery Goods
Drugs	Paints, Oils, Glass
Dry Goods	Stationery
Fancy Goods	Tea
Fruits	Tobacco
Groceries	Watches and Jewelry
Hardware	Wines and Liquor

The possibilities for concentration on a particular line of products by wholesale merchants increased in direct relation to the increase in the size of the markets. A second factor encouraging such specialization, and one with a closer causal relationship, was the increasing degree of specialization among the retailers to whom the wholesaler's sales were made, which in turn, of course, depended upon the degree of industrialization and urbanization and so was a more important factor after the Civil War than in 1860.

The wholesale merchants who sold domestic goods only were probably far outnumbered by those who relied on a combination of domestic and imported goods for sale. In the hardware trade, for

example, practically the entire stock of most merchants was
imported. A prominent wholesale hardware salesman writes that:

> Nearly all the purchases of the house were
> English or German goods, for at that time [1860]
> the American hardware manufacturers had not
> begun to produce those fine and cheap wares
> which have won for us our own market....[44]

The lack of availability of American made hardware probably had
little more influence on the decision by wholesalers to concentrate
inventories on imports than did market considerations. There was a
general prejudice on the part of retail buyers against domestic
hardware which only a superior product coupled with time and good
sales strategy finally overcame.[45] It is true, however, that by
1860 there was a noticeable trend among wholesale merchants to
include in their inventories increasing proportions of American
manufactures as they became available.

Even in the hardware trade, one of the last strongholds for the
sale of imports, there were some wholesale merchants devoting
themselves almost entirely to the sale of American made goods before
the Civil War.[46] There were dealers in toys and watches advertising
as handling American made goods exclusively. In other lines such as
boots and shoes and groceries the importing of goods had never been
so extensive as in hardware. It appears also that the number of
wholesale merchants in a given trade handling domestic goods
exclusively, as well as the proportion of domestic goods found in
the inventories of those handling both foreign and American made

goods, was influenced directly by the progress made in manufacturing in these lines in the United States.

The extension of credit. One of the major problems faced by these wholesale merchants lay in the granting of credit. The terms were long, the information upon which a credit decision had to be based was often unreliable and, consequently, the bad debt losses were large in relation to sales. In commenting editorially on the financial failure of a New York dry goods wholesaler the Tribune termed it a "common practice" in 1860 to sell large orders to southern firms of no known capital "nominally on twelve months time but really on fourteen or fifteen months, as the goods are sold and delivered in February and the notes at twelve months dated the first of April ensuing."[47] Similar terms were offered in the hardware trade in the South where most of the volume was sold on terms of twelve months.[48]

The credit period in the South was longer generally than in the North because of the difference in the economic structures of the two areas. The South, built on an agricultural base, was forced to adjust its credit terms to crop harvests leading to the twelve month periods which were deplored by many of the more progressive merchants in the North and West. In the latter areas credits were not so long, generally running about six months on the average, although terms varied for different trades. In the North, hardware, for example, was sold largely on credit, the notes running from four

to eight months.[49] The credit period in the East was shorter,
usually, than that in the South, and in the West it was shorter
still. Although it was not unusual for a firm to advertise price
inducements to obtain cash no instances of the use of the cash
discount as it is presently used were found. This was apparently a
post-Civil War development.

The Panic of 1857 brought about the failure of some firms
because of over-extended credit. It also brought about a general
tightening in credit granting policy, especially in the West. In
the Chicago dry goods market, for example, shortened credits and
prompt pay were emphasized in 1859 and resulted in greater ease in
making collections.[50] The Panic, coupled with a minor recession in
1860, seems to have given increased impetus to the movement in the
direction of shorter credit periods and more stringent terms
generally. The difference between the East and West though was
still marked and is illustrated in the following account:

> It is a fact, which may seem strange, that
> there are many merchants doing business in
> various towns in the Western States, who can buy
> as much Dry Goods in Eastern Cities as they
> please, and yet whose credit at home is, in many
> instances, second class and in not a few
> absolutely worthless. The ease with which, and
> upon what a slender basis, a credit of fifty to
> one hundred thousand dollars can be established
> in New York, say, has become proverbial out
> west, and bear a striking contrast with the care
> and scrutiny used by our merchants.[51]

The reason for the greater liberality in credit in the East as
contrasted with Western centers was no doubt largely based on

competitive considerations because it was at this time that much
Western trade was being lured away from the East by the inland
centers. A recurring difficulty faced by the wholesale merchant was
the problem of securing good credit information. The establishment
in 1841 and subsequent rapid growth of the mercantile agencies
helped to overcome this eventually. However, in 1860 much reliance
was still placed on personal introductions, information from other
sellers, and information furnished by traveling salesmen as a basis
for credit decisions. Salesmen were relatively few in 1860 and
although much of their time was taken up with credit investigation
this source was far from adequate. The houses with which the
customer formerly dealt were sometimes asked to supply credit
information and they were not above recommending the customer so he
could get the means with which to pay them. The mercantile agencies
were not reliable in some cases.[52] All of this led to a very
serious problem for the wholesale merchant in which little progress
was made until after the Civil War. Although the undesirability of
long credit had been recognized and the trend toward a shorter
period had started by 1860, much remained to be done thereafter.

Traveling salesmen. As indicated much of the time of the early
traveling salesman was spent in gathering credit information and he
was expected to evaluate and determine the desirability of a
customer as a credit risk.[53] It is probable that this practice was
an outgrowth of the early employment of commercial travelers as

collectors who occasionally took an order but whose main purpose was to collect for goods previously sold. With the gradual shift from a sellers' to a buyers' market and increasing competition it would seem only logical for the emphasis on the commercial traveler's work to shift from collecting to selling, the gathering of credit information and collection of accounts now incidental to the sales activity. The use of salesmen as reporters of credit information and collectors of accounts still persists to some extent today.

There were very few traveling salesmen in 1860, probably not more than 1,000, and nearly all were from eastern cities.[54] Traveling representatives had been sent out to solicit business for their firms as early as 1803 and isolated instances of their use exist in the 1830's and 40's.[55] However, traveling salesmen were not commonly employed until after the Civil War.

The prevailing practice, even in 1860 when some traveling men were used, was for the merchants to come to the markets twice a year where they were met by the salesmen, or drummers, and conducted to the salesrooms. That this practice was widespread and had become quite an art is indicated in the following:

> The buyers would come to New York in great droves twice a year to replenish their stocks, and this was the drummers' great opportunity. A country merchant would want Dry Goods, Boots and Shoes, Hardware, Drugs, Groceries, etc. An agreement or compact would be formed between, say, half a dozen jobbing firms, all representing distinctly different lines. A suite of rooms would be rented and fitted up in comfortable shape, with ample accommodations for

> eating, drinking and smoking...and drummers from
> different houses in the compact would watch the
> hotel registers for their prey. A dry goods
> drummer, for instance, would light on a man and
> introduce him to the drummers in all the lines
> of trade represented in the compact. He would
> be dined, wined, smoked, theatred, etc., and
> most carefully kept in tow until all the houses
> in the arrangement had a crack at him, with the
> result that nine times out of ten he would
> purchase all his supplies from the houses
> represented in the association and the only real
> competition was one association of merchants
> working against another association of like
> character.[56]

From such a practice it is only a step to sending the drummer out to

call on the customer instead of waiting for him to come to the

market where he would be subjected to pressures from competitors on

all sides.

The Western wholesalers were distinctly unhappy over the use of

traveling salemen by their Eastern competitors. These merchants

proceeded to forecast the downfall of those employing salesmen and

probably played a major role in the passing of laws in some states

and municipalities prohibiting non-resident sellers from operating

in these areas without a license. A prominent Chicago dry goods

wholesaler writing in 1859 stated that the practice of Eastern

merchants of operating their businesses with "runners, is, to use a

trite phrase 'run into the ground'" and he gloomily forecast for the

Eastern merchants that their losses from the use of salesmen would

be equivalent to the losses suffered by them in over-extending

Western credit.[57] Briggs states that about the time of the Civil

War there were laws requiring the licensing of commercial travelers in such cities as Washington, D.C., Savannah, St. Louis, and Chicago, the fees ranging from $50 to $100 per year.[58] The fact that many of these laws were repealed as soon as the merchants in those towns having license ordinances began to send out salesmen of their own would seem to bear out the conclusion above that some of the laws, at least, were passed as competitive devices at the instance of the local business interests.

Although the traveling salesmen in 1860 were relatively few in numbers, poorly trained, inadequately compensated and supervised, they were, nevertheless, proving their economic worth and establishing a place for themselves in the wholesale merchants' organization and in the economic scheme of things.

The difficulties met by these early salesmen were magnified because of the lack of fixed prices. Prices were widely quoted in many trades on the basis of a discount from list and the salesmen exercised considerable latitude in varying the amount of the discount to meet the situation. Correspondence from salesmen to their home offices frequently contained complaints that competitive salesmen were cutting prices and gave this as a reason for their having booked orders at less than the minimum desirable price.[59] It is probable that these early travelers spent considerable time in negotiating prices and that the quotations varied markedly between customers at any given time. An examination of advertisements in

contemporary newspapers and directories indicates almost no cases
where the price of goods was advertised in any but general terms,
"prices as low as any in the trade" being a common expression. It
is obvious that such a system gave rise to abuses and
misunderstandings which could have been avoided with a one-price
system. Such a system, with various modifications, eventually
developed after the War.

Advertising. Not only was there little or no mention of
prices in advertisements, there was little advertising of specific
products. The advertisements were practically all simple
announcements of the kind and location of the firm with an
occasional bit of copy urging potential customers to call. The
emphasis upon brands in advertising by manufacturers was not strong
and was practically non-existent in the case of wholesalers. The
use of distributors' brands was an innovation of the 1870's. This
is not difficult to understand when one considers the status of
wholesalers at this time. In many lines they were small
non-specialized firms without the resources to handle their own
brands. Although competition was intense it was to become more
severe both among wholesalers, and between wholesalers and
manufacturers selling direct which gave the former more incentive to
discover and apply new competitive techniques. This will be
analyzed further in connection with the discussion of the rise of
distributors' brands.

Organization of the wholesale firm. The bulk of the business
of wholesale merchants in 1860 was carried on by partnerships. Some
firms operated as single proprietorships but these seem to have been
in the minority. The corporate form of organization in wholesaling
did not develop to any extent until later. Documentation for this
point is provided by the firm signatures in contemporary
advertisements and in the histories of the firms then in existence.
Contemporary or early historians and writers in business almost
invariably devoted a great deal of space to a description of the
succession of partners active in the firm over the years.[60]
Advertisements not infrequently contained the names of several
partners and, on occasion, a statement of the present firm's
predecessor. The latter included presumably because of a recent
change in partners bringing about a change in the firm name.

This absence of incorporations was due to circumstances under
which the wholesale firm operated. Its business, even compared with
those of the next decade or two, was not large and sufficient
capital could usually be provided by partners' funds and their
credit. The actual operation did not require a complex
organization of authority and responsibility:

> In the early days the proprietors of the
> Hardware jobbing houses did most of the work
> themselves; but few letters had to be written;
> no traveling men had to be looked after, and the
> proprietors usually after selling a bill of
> hardware got it out, had it packed and shipped,
> and made out the invoice themselves. This
> custom to a great extent was still in vogue when
> I entered the hardware business in 1878.[61]

This statement is applicable not only in hardware, which ultimately led in incorporations of individual firms, but to varying degrees in most of the other trades. This is not meant to imply that there were no wholesalers with large organizations. The fact is, however, that it remained for increasing competition, widening markets, and the resultant necessity of more complex and closely controlled operations to bring about the well-knit organizations which were to grow in the later decades of the century.

Shipping Merchants, Importers and Exporters

In the leading seaports in 1860 there operated a class of merchant middlemen known as shipping merchants. Shipping merchants carried on a general importing and exporting business and owned the ships in which the merchandise were transported.[62]

There appears to have been less specialization by this class of intermediary than among some of the other middlemen. Before the Civil War the typical shipping merchant often operated as an agent as well as a merchant middleman. The New York directory of 1864, for example, lists 269 individuals and firms operating in New York City as shipping and commission merchants.[63] There were also a number of firms classified as shipping and importing merchants. The shipping merchants were likely to operate wherever there were possibilities of profit. One firm advertised itself as shipping and commission merchants, and foreign exchange and emigration agents.[64]

There apparently were no firms at this time engaged exclusively
in exporting. The reason probably was that the volume of American
exports had not yet reached a point where specialization was
profitable. The export business was handled by the shipping
merchants, manufacturers, and agents of foreign firms.[65]

There was a considerable degree of specialization by products
among importers. There were importers who advertised themselves as
specializing in such commodities as dry goods, china and glass,
hardware, paper hangings, watches, wines, and drugs and chemicals.
The degree of specialization was probably carried further in dry
goods than in any other single line. Prior to the Civil War there
were dry goods importers who specialized in China and India goods,
cloths, cassimeres and vestings, linen, silk and fancy dry goods,
and woolen goods.[66]

Many importers advertised that they sold at both wholesale and
retail. It is not uncommon to find in the 1860 business directories
advertisements stating that a firm engaged in importing and
wholesaling of a particular class of goods. Others advertised that
they were importers and dealers, importers, manufacturers, and
dealers, or importers and jobbers in certain lines.

It is clear that the shipping merchants and importers were
numerous and carrying on extensive operations in 1860. Some of the
importing firms maintained representatives in foreign markets
looking after their interests there. It was reported of the
Philadelphia dry goods trade in 1859 that:

> With respect to <u>Foreign Dry Goods</u>, the import-
> ting houses of Philadelphia certainly possess the
> same facilities for procuring desirable selections
> on advantageous terms as any others do; and in some
> instances enjoy unusually favorable connections in
> Europe established long since, and by means of
> these secure perhaps more than their share of
> bargains. The stocks are generally selected by
> resident partners, who know the wants and consult
> the interests of purchasers; and therefore they
> consist, less than some others, of the unsalable
> refuse of London warehouses.[67]

Similarly some of the shipping merchants also had representatives abroad in order to maintain close contact with the markets.

The situation in which these middlemen were operating was dynamic and considerable change took place subsequent to 1860 in their status and operations. These changes and the reasons why they took place will be examined in Chapter IV.

Agent Middlemen in Operation in 1860

It has been pointed out that some of these middlemen operated both as agent and merchant wholesalers. There were also those, in most of the major markets, who operated strictly as agent wholesalers. Among these were auctioneers, brokers, and factors or commission merchants. According to the census in 1860 there were in the United States and territories 1,348 auctioneers, 4,907 brokers, and 3,952 commission merchants.[68]

<u>Auctioneers</u>. Auctions began to decline in relative importance before 1860 and this trend was to continue throughout the remainder of the century. Changing economic conditions and modes of doing

business were largely responsible for the decreasing prominence of auctions in the wholesale system. More specifically there were five major causes which were operative by 1860 in reducing the relative importance of this marketing institution.[69]

1. Buyers often preferred to buy privately because this made it possible to get the long credits they needed.

2. Textile selling agents were operating more and more aggressively so fewer textiles were being sold at auctions.

3. Improvements in transportation and communications made it easier for foreign agents to contact and sell directly to the wholesalers quantities of good formerly sold at auction.

4. Development of interior cities as wholesale centers attracted many merchants who formerly attended the large auctions in the eastern centers.

5. Brokers were beginning to handle many goods which formerly went through auctions.

It is true, nevertheless, that in absolute terms large quantities of goods were still being distributed by this means in 1860. The duties collected in New York in that year amounted to $125,929.83,[70] when the duties upon goods sold at auction ranged from one-half to one percent with all domestic goods, other than liquors, specifically excepted.[71] This indicates a volume of sales, in foreign goods and domestic liquors alone, in the neighborhood of fifteen to twenty million dollars. About 257 auctioneers were active in this market, that was roughly 20 percent of the total number operative in the United States.

The auctioneers were, in most cases, closely regulated by the states and municipalities in which they operated.[72] In New York, Boston, Philadelphia, Chicago, and St. Louis, for example auctioneers were prohibited from operating without first obtaining a license, the fee ranging from $2 per year in Boston to not less than $500 in Philadelphia. With the exception of Boston duties of one-fourth to one and one-half percent were levied on the auctioneer's sales in these cities and, in all cases, they were required to furnish a bond and to make a quarterly report of sales.[73] Other provisions varied but it is apparent from the examples that the auctions were closely regulated, although there seems to have been some tendency toward relaxation in these regulations by 1860. Advertisements in contemporary newspapers indicated auctioneers were especially active in the sale of dry goods, groceries, boots and shoes, furniture, and stationery and books, of which the advertisements of the sale of dry goods at auction were most numerous.[74]

Commission merchants. The most numerous of the agent wholesalers were the commission merchants, or factors, of which over one-half were located in the five states of Virginia, Louisiana,

Ohio, Illinois, and New York. The latter alone accounted for almost one-fourth of the total. Factors were then defined as:

> A person or agent, frequently resident in a foreign country, employed by third parties to transact business on their own account. A factor differs in some respects from an ordinary agent or broker, as they most frequently have merely to sell or buy the goods in the name of the principal, while the factor has possession of the goods and frequently advances money upon or sells them, without necessarily disclosing the name of his principal or person employing him.[75]

It was very common in 1860 to find the commission merchant combining more than one type of operation. Advertisements showed that very often he acted also as a wholesale merchant of one type or another. The combination of commission merchant and wholesale grocer was not unusual; nor was that of forwarding and commission merchant. The forwarding function, however, was declining in importance with the increasing availability of through transportation. This would seem to account for the secondary emphasis on this function in the directory and newspaper advertisements by the agents operating in that dual capacity.

Although most of the commission merchants seem to have been engaged in a general commission business there were those who specialized in:[76]

Cotton	Oil
Drugs	Paper
Dry Goods	Produce
Glass and Glassware	Tea and Tobacco
Grain	Wool
Lumber	

The functions performed by these middlemen can be grouped under the general headings of selling and purchasing goods and supplies, and the financial activities involved in supplying funds and credits to principals. The commissions charged for these services constituted the major sources of the revenue received by the commission merchant. For those who combined commission and merchant operations, however, there was additional revenue accruing in the purchase of supplies for the principal. This was particularly important in the South where the factor handled practically all the supplies used on the plantations.

Brokers. Some of the same forces working to the detriment of auctions were benefitting brokers. Though there had been few brokers in 1860 they were relatively numerous by the forties and the auctioneers of New York in 1849 cited increased sales through brokers as a reason for the decline in auction duties.[77] By 1860 brokers were firmly entrenched in the distribution structure. An insight into their position is provided by a definition from Banker's Magazine:

> Brokers.--Persons employed as middlemen between producers or sellers of any commodity, and buyers or consumers. The principal are Bill Brokers, Stock Brokers, Ship and Insurance Brokers. But many other of the most important trades have brokers, who confine their attention exclusively to such particular branches, as silk, sugar, indigo, etc.; and whose intervention it is desirable to employ, and trustworthiness of the leading buyers, and other reasons. A broker, unlike a factor, only sells by sample, and does not hold possession of the goods.[78]

This is substantially the same definition employed today in speaking of brokers and indicated a considerable degree of development among these agents by 1860. The latter part of the definition shows a recognition of the value of the services of merchandise brokers in providing market information. This was no doubt especially significant in accounting for the rapid growth in relative importance of brokers, particularly in view of the limitations of the existing systems of transportation and communication.

The definition indicates that there were merchandise brokers specializing in silk, sugar, and indigo. To this could be added many more lines; for example, the Boston Almanac for 1860 lists fifty-six merchandise brokers, thirteen of whom specialized in indigo, flour, wool, metal, hides, lumber, cotton, and tea. No specialty was listed for the remainder. There were also brokers in other markets who specialized in produce, drugs, horses, oil, grain, hay, and tobacco. It is difficult to determine the total number of merchandise brokers in the United States in that year since the census figure of 4,907 includes all types of brokers. It is apparent, however, that by 1860 the merchandise broker was taking a position as an important cog in the distributive machinery and was operating much as he does today.

Commissions. The rates of commission varied with the type of transactions involved. An indication of the varied functions performed by these agents and brokers is contained in the following statement of the New York Chamber of Commerce recommending the commissions to be charged where no express agreement to the contrary existed.[79]

Banking	Percent
On purchase of stocks, bonds and all kinds of securities....	1
On sale of stocks, bonds and all kinds of securities........	1
On purchase or sale of specie and bullion...................	1/2
Remittances in bills of exchange............................	1/2
Remittances in bills of exchange, with guarantee............	1
Collecting dividends on stocks and other securities.........	1/2
Collecting interest on bonds and mortgages..................	1

General Business

On sales of sugar, coffee, tea and general merchandise, usually sold in large quantities, and on credits under six months or for cash....................................	5
On sales of goods usually sold on long credits, for commissions and guarantee.................................	7 1/2
On sales of manufactured goods and other articles usually sold for cash...	5
On purchase and shipment of merchandise with funds in hand, on cost and charges.................................	2 1/2
Collecting delayed and litigated accounts...................	5
Effecting marine insurance, on amount insured..............	1/2
Receiving and forwarding merchandise, on invoice value one percent and on expenses incurred......................	2 1/2

Shipping

On purchase or sale of vessels..............................	2 1/2
Disbursements and outfit of vessels.........................	2 1/2
Procuring freight...	5
Collecting freight...	2 1/2
Collecting insurance losses of all kinds...................	2 1/2

The agent middlemen with their broad and varied operations occupied a place of prominence in the distribution structure in 1860. However, there were economic and institutional forces gathering which were destined to alter both their relative positions and methods of operation in ensuing decades.

Summary

It is clear that by 1860 there had been developed in the United States, in response to changing economic conditions, a relatively elaborate wholesaling structure. The foundations of many of the more important present-day wholesale institutions had been or were being laid by that time.

The large centers which had dominated trade from their coastal locations were being seriously challenged by the new centers developing along the natural waterways of the interior. The railroad net, developing with increased rapidity, was bringing many of the formerly more or less isolated market centers into closer relationship with each other. It was also opening up new areas of settlement, creating new markets, and new arenas of competition. Although the so-called national market did not yet exist there was emerging a pattern upon which it was to be woven in the following decades.

The environment of the wholesaler at this time was change, brought on by the increasing industrialization and urbanization and the improvements which were being wrought in transportation and communications. The older channel of importer-jobber-retailer-consumer was giving way to that of manufacturer-wholesaler-retailer-consumer as the most important route to the markets. Many wholesalers were availing themselves of the economies of specialization by function as well as by product lines. The auction, as an important marketing institution, was giving way to newer types of agent middlemen such as brokers and manufacturers' agents. If cotton was king in the south the factor was the power behind the throne, although his position, too, was to be radically altered in the next four decades. The entire structure of wholesale markets and the system of middlemen operative in those markets was in a state of transition.

The problems encountered by these middlemen were many and varied. Some were difficulties faced by the entire economy; others were peculiar to the wholesale organization. The prevalence of the attitude of "Caveat Emptor" led to inefficiencies and losses. The credit problems were serious because of a lack of reliable credit information, and were further complicated by instability in the existing systems of currency and banking. The lack of knowledge of good accounting, control, organization, and other internal business procedures resulted in losses which were later avoided. Of course, it is true that the relative simplicity of business organization and operation made a knowledge of these factors less essential at this time than later.

Absence of good market information, high cost and limited transportation, poor packing, and so on, were factors which further complicated the wholesaler's business operations. In retrospect some of these problems would appear to be readily soluble. Viewed in their proper perspective and correct frame of reference, however, they were not as obviously soluble. The efforts by wholesalers to overcome these and other difficulties, coupled with the changing economic, governmental, and social environment, played a significant part in shaping the present wholesale structure.

FOOTNOTES – CHAPTER II

[1] *Report of the National Conservation Commission* (Washington, 1909), II, pp. 57-8.

[2] *One Hundred Years Progress of the United States* (Hartford, Conn: L. Stebbins, 1872), p. 159.

[3] For estimates from 1899 to 1935 see N. R. Engle, "An Estimate of the Volume of Wholesale Trade in the United States, 1899-1935," *Survey of Current Business*, May, 1935, U.S. Bureau of Foreign and Domestic Commerce.

[4] *Southern Historical Publications Society*, "The South in the Building of the Nation," 1909, Vol. 5, p. 408.

[5] E.L. Bogart and D.L. Kemmerer, *Economic History of the American People* (New York: Longmanns, Green and Co., 1949), p. 302.

[6] John H. Frederick, *The Development of American Commerce* (New York: D. Appleton and Company, 1932), p. 104.

[7] G.W. Baker, *A Review of the Relative Commercial Progress of the Cities of New York and Philadelphia* (Philadelphia, 1859), p. 18.

[8] Stephen Colwell, *The Five Cotton States and New York* (1861), p. 23.

[9] *Ibid.*, p. 27.

[10] *Eighth Census of Manufactures*, 1860.

[11] *Hunt's Merchant Magazine*, Vol. XXXXII (1860), p. 610.

[12] Boston Board of Trade, *Fifth Annual Report* (Boston, 1859), p. 179.

[13] Boston Board of Trade, *Fourth Annual Report*, p. 86.

[14] Boston Board of Trade, *Third Annual Report*, p. 107.

[15] Philadelphia Board of Trade, *Twenty-Seventh Annual Report* (Philadelphia, 1860), p. 35.

[16] *Op. cit.*, p. 38.

[17] See R.G. Albion, *The Rise of the New York Port* (New York, 1939).

[18] Quoted in *Hunt's Merchant Magazine*, Vol. XXXXII (1860), p. 565.

[19]Quoted in De Bow's Review, Vol. XXVIII (1860), p. 331.

[20]De Bow's Review, Vol. XXVII (1860), p. 33.

[21]U.S. House Executive Documents, 50th Congress, 1st Session, 1887-88, Vol. 20, Report on the Internal Commerce of the United States, p. 213.

[22]Ibid., p. 214.

[23]Charles Cist, Sketches and Statistics of Cincinnati in 1859 (Cincinnati, 1859), p. 346.

[24]Loc. cit.

[25]Ibid., p. 347.

[26]William Smith, Annual Statement of the Trade and Commerce of Cincinnati (Cincinnati, 1859), p. 15.

[27]Chicago Board of Trade, Third Annual Statement of the Trade and Commerce of Chicago for Year Ending December 31st, 1860 (Chicago, 1861), p. 56.

[28]Chicago Press and Tribune, January 12, 1860, p. 2.

[29]A.T. Andreas, History of Chicago (Chicago, 1884), Vol. III, p. 716.

[30]J. Moses and J. Kirkland, eds., The History of Chicago, Illinois (Chicago, 1859), Vol. I, p. 288.

[31]Ibid., p. 292.

[32]Ibid., p. 297.

[33]Loc. cit.

[34]J.S. Wright, Chicago: Past, Present and Future (Chicago, 1860).

[35]John Hogan, Thoughts about the City of St. Louis (St. Louis, 1854), p. 3.

[36]I.H. Lionberger, The Annals of St. Louis (St. Louis, Missouri Historical Society, 1929), p. 73.

[37]W.B. Stevens, St. Louis, the Fourth City, 1764-1911 (St. Louis, 1911), p. 469.

[38]Loc. cit.

[39]J.H. Hollander, The Cincinnati Southern Railway (Baltimore, 1894), p. 13.

[40]Ben Casseday, The History of Louisville (Louisville, 1852), p. 234.

[41]Louisville Board of Trade, Annual Report for the Year Ending March 31st, 1867 (Louisville, 1867), p. 18.

[42]Eighth Census of Manufactures, 1860, p. lxxii.

[43]Fred M. Jones, "The Development of Marketing Channels in the United States to 1920" (unpublished manuscript, College of Commerce, University of Illinois, Urbana), p. 14.

[44]E.P. Briggs, Fifty Years on the Road (Philadelphia, 1911), p. 12.

[45]Samuel A. Bigelow, "Fifty Years in the Hardware Business," Iron Age (January 4, 1906), p. 151.

[46]J.E. Bishop, A History of American Manufactures (Philadelphia, 1866), Vol. II, p. 386.

[47]New York Daily Tribune, October 17, 1860, p. 2.

[48]B.F. Eshleman, "The South Fifty Years Ago," Iron Age, January 4, 1906, p. 166.

[49]B.P. Briggs, op. cit., p. 34.

[50]A.T. Andreas, op. cit., p. 716.

[51]William Smith, Annual Statement of the Trade and Commerce of Cincinnati (Cincinnati, 1859), p. 18.

[52]Briggs, op. cit., p. 127.

[53]Ibid., p. 52.

[54]Ibid.

[55]Fred M. Jones, "Middlemen in the Domestic Trade of the United States, 1800-1860," Illinois Studies in the Social Sciences, Vol. XXI, No. 3, p. 16.

[56]A.H. Saxton, "Jobbing Trade Fifty Years Ago," Iron Age, January 4, 1906, p. 149.

[57]Chicago Board of Trade, Second Annual Statement of the Trade and Commerce of Chicago (Chicago, 1860), p. 75.

[58]Briggs, op. cit., p. 48.

[59]For an early example of this see T.F. Marburg, "Manufacturer's Drummer, 1852," Bulletin of the Business Historical Society, Vol. XXII, No. 3 (June, 1948), p. 106.

[60]See, for example, Andreas, op. cit., pp. 694-5.

[61]R.M. Dudley, "The Hardware Trade of the South," Iron Age, January 4, 1906, p. 154.

[62]G.W. Sheldon, "Old Shipping Merchants of New York City," Harper's Monthly, February, 1892, Vol. 84, p. 457.

[63]New York State Business Directory, 1864, pp. 139-41.

[64]Ibid., pp. 140, 851.

[65]Fred M. Jones, "The Development of Marketing Channels in the United States to 1920," op. cit., p. 14.

[66]See, for example, Boston Directory, 1860, and New York State Business Directory, 1864.

[67]E.T. Freedley, Philadelphia and Its Manufactures (Philadelphia, 1859), p. 96.

[68]Eighth Census of Population, 1860, pp. 656-67.

[69]Jones, "Middlemen in the Domestic Trade of the United States, 1800-1860," op. cit., pp. 39-40.

[70]New York Assembly Documents, 1878, No. 64.

[71]New York State Laws Relating to the City of New York, 1862, p. 298.

[72]For discussions of the evolution of this legislation leading up to 1860 see R.B. Westerfield, "Early History of American Auctions," Transactions of the Connecticut Academy of Arts and Science, Vol. 23, pp. 199-208; Jones, op. cit., pp. 40-3.

[73]Brown, Philadelphia Digest, 1701-1904, pp. 883-94; City of St. Louis Ordinances, 1856, pp. 198-9; New York State Laws Relating to the City of New York, 1862, pp. 297-310; Boston Laws and Ordinances 1864, pp. 35-7; Charter and Ordinances of Chicago, Sept. 15, 1856 inclusive, pp. 164-6.

[74]See, for example, New York Herald, 1860 and Cincinnati Commercial, 1861.

[75]Banker's Mazazine, Vol. X (New Series), January, 1861, p. 556.

[76]From an examination of William's Cincinnati Directory, 1860; Adams and Sampson, Boston Directory, 1860; Central New York Business Directory, 1861; New York Daily Tribune and the Cincinnati Commercial for 1860.

[77]Jones, op. cit., pp. 26-7.

[78]Banker's Magazine, op. cit., pp. 550-1.

[79]New York Chamber of Commerce, Annual Report for the Year 1858 (New York 1859), p. 243.

cf. Philadelphia Board of Trade, Twenty-Eighth Annual Report (Philadelphia, 1861), pp. 137-8 and Jones, op. cit., p. 23.

CHAPTER III

GROWTH AND DEVELOPMENT OF WHOLESALE TRADING CENTERS, 1860-1900

The purpose of the present chapter is to examine the changes which took place in the system of wholesale market centers between 1860 and 1900. During this period national development proceeded at a rapid pace. The Civil War itself marked the end of an era and was a turning-point in the economic and business history of the country. Many of the fundamental economic, political, and social changes which occurred in the forty years following 1860 played a major role in the subsequent growth and development of the wholesaler, his markets, and the general business environment in which he operated.

It is not possible to examine carefully and fully comprehend the development of the wholesale middlemen and the wholesale marketing centers between 1860 and 1900 without some knowledge of the economic changes which took place during that period as a frame of reference against which to set the analysis. Therefore, it is worthwhile to pause briefly, before proceeding into the specific examination of the development of wholesale centers, to outline some of the more important of these basic considerations. Others will be brought into the discussion and detail added as the occasion arises.

Economic Setting

What, then, were some of the factors and forces which exerted so much influence on the evolution of the wholesaling structure? Of primary importance was the rapidly expanding population. In 1860 the

population of the continental United States was 31,441,321 and by

1900 it had more than doubled, reaching 76,303,387. This fact alone

would account for a rapid expansion in wholesaling but just as

important were the effects of the urbanization and westward movement

of the population. The number of people living in urban areas and

the number and the size of cities increased very rapidly during this

period. The westward movement continued and new towns and cities

were established in the West. It is true that the rate of increase

in population was not as large as it had been before 1860 but the

increase in density of population was greater than ever before.

Furthermore, there was a distinct movement during this period from

the self-sufficient toward the inter-dependent type of economic and

social organization. Many of these changes were to have both a

beneficial and an adverse effect on the wholesaler and his marketing

operations as will be shown later.

The railroad net, a second factor of importance, was virtually

completed during this period and served to link the system of markets

together. The railroad enlarged the area which could be served by

the major wholesale centers and aided in the exploitation and

settlement of new areas which became fertile markets for the goods

handled by wholesalers. At the same time this railroad net brought

the wholesale centers and their middlemen into closer competition

with each other. Nevertheless, by 1860 the railroad had demonstrated its superiority as a means of transportation and, in the ensuing period, was to be instrumental in radically altering the relative positions of some of the larger market centers and the routes over which their trade moved. The railroad was both a cause and an offset in the economic development of these decades and its influence on the development of the wholesaler is not easily over-emphasized.

Another of the significant factors of this period was the rapid growth in manufacturing. The products of manufacturing rose from $1.8 billion in 1860 to $13 billion in 1900. Again it will become apparent that this development, though producing obvious stimuli to the growth of wholesaling middlemen and centers, was not an unmixed blessing as far as the wholesalers were concerned in the later decades.

As previously noted, the prevalence of a sellers' market before the Civil War and the subsequent change to a buyers' market thereafter is a generally accepted fact. This led to increasing competition both between markets and among the individual wholesale firms operating in a particular market. It also contributed to business difficulties during this period and undoubtedly lent considerable impetus to the tendency to combine and integrate which was apparent in most lines of business.

A factor closely related to the above in its effects was the generally declining price level. Chart I is a representation of wholesale prices and their fluctuations during this period. From a

low in 1860 wholesale prices rose rapidly till 1864 and then declined
almost steadily until 1896 when the trend was reversed and again
became upward. Exceptions to the downward trend were in 1871 and
1872, a period of mixed prosperity, and again in 1878-82 which was a
period of revival and prosperity following the Panic of 1873.

Table III summarizes the stages of the business cycle by dates
and will be referred to in the discussion below. It is apparent that
the period was not without obstacles to the growth and development of
wholesaling. Generally speaking, however, it was one of rapid growth
for the wholesale centers and middlemen. The two decades preceding
1900 seem to have been especially prosperous ones for the wholesalers
in spite of the movement which took place at that time to eliminate
some of the middlemen and shorten the channels of distribution.

During the period under consideration, then, it appears that
the major requisites necessary to the development of an extensive
system of wholesale markets and middlemen were present. The center
of a continually growing population was moving westward opening new
areas to trade. The aggregate volume of production, especially
manufacturing, increased many fold; the wealth of the country rose
even faster than the population and the efficiency of transportation
was being continually increased. These factors, along with ever
increasing inter-regional interdependency and diversity of
production, combined to produce an environment which was favorable to
the development and enlargement of the wholesale structure.

CHART I

INDEX OF WHOLESALE PRICES, 1860-1900

(1910-14=100)

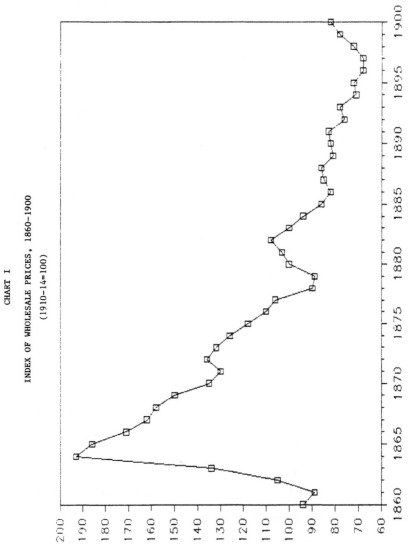

Source: Warren, G.F., and Pearson, F.A., Prices (New York: John Wiley and Sons, 1933), pp. 11-13.

TABLE III

BUSINESS FLUCTUATIONS IN THE UNITED STATES, 1860-1900

Revival	Prosperity	Recession	Depression
1859	1860	1860	1861
1861	1862-65	1865	1866-67
1868	1869	1870	
1871	1872-73	1873	1874-78
1878-79	1880-82	1882-83	1884-85
1885-86	1887	1888	
1888	1889-90	1890	1891
1891	1892	1893	1893-95
1895		1896	1896-97
1897-98	1898-1900		

Source: W.L. Thorp, Business Annals (New York: National Bureau of
Economic Research, 1926), pp. 77-81.

The remainder of the present discussion will be devoted to an examination of the effect of these and other more specific factors on the growth of wholesale marketing centers during the period 1860 to 1900.

Changing Relative Importance of Wholesale Market Centers

Throughout this period the major centers referred to earlier continued, in absolute terms, to expand and enlarge their facilities and spheres of influence. Relatively, however, the situation was quite different. It is apparent from the previous discussion that as early as 1860 some of the older centers were declining in the face of competition from the newer, more progressive and richly endowed markets. This relative change continued after 1860 and was accentuated by the Civil War, the trend toward highly specialized localized industry, improvements in transportation, and by the natural advantages in location and economic resources possessed by some of the centers.

Increasing numbers of jobbing points were being established in the smaller cities and towns throughout the interior and western United States. The smaller cities situated along the rivers were in an especially advantageous position to receive the quantity shipments from the East and to break them up into smaller lots for sale to the country merchants. Many of these points were established in response to the changing economic conditions referred to above. Furthermore, as the market widened with increasing population and improved rail

transportation facilities, centers were set up in towns other than
those along the rivers and coasts. Wholesale operations were carried
on at these points by newly established firms, by retailers assuming
a jobbing function, and by wholesalers from the larger cities
establishing branch houses in order to be nearer the market and thus
meet local competition more effectively.

The changing relative importance of the older wholesale
centers, the establishment of new ones, and the development of the
railroad all contributed to the modification of the tradiational
lines of trade. Where, as shown above, the primary currents of trade
had been largely a case of North—South movement before 1860, this was
now changed to become East—West. The simplicity which characterized
the situation in 1860 was rapidly replaced by a complex,
inter—related system. This becomes particularly apparent in
examining the structure of wholesale centers during the period under
consideration.

The Two Leading Centers, New York and Chicago

New York. The largest of the wholesale centers in 1860 was New
York. Since it continued to occupy the dominant position throughout
the ensuing decades it provides a good point of departure in
analyzing the further development of wholesale marketing centers.
Such an analysis logically proceeds with a consideration of the
change in the size, composition, and relative importance of the

centers, the factors which influenced their growth and development, and the effect of this upon the wholesalers and their operations.

Throughout this period New York was unquestionably the most important link in the chain of wholesale centers which supplied the needs of the country. Although New York, with its unexcelled water transportation facilities, developed slowly as a railroad center a tremendous expansion in railroads tributary to the city took place after 1860 and it maintained its superiority in this new phase of transportation development.

It is difficult to quantify the amount of wholesale trade of the city since no reliable data are available. An idea of the development of New York as a trade center, however, can be derived from merchandise import and export figures which are available for the period under consideration:[1]

	Imports	Exports*
1860	$229,408,130	$ 95,468,296
1865	222,619,138	174,247,454
1870	303,335,378	185,740,061
1875	327,190,362	247,681,724
1880	464,176,680	406,955,884
1885	383,540,456	321,149,580
1890	542,366,488	339,458,578
1895	516,286,774	323,402,003
1900	526,106,781	526,153,270

By 1900 there were 4,653 wholesale merchants and dealers in New York City. The number of agents was 23,704.** Thus about 10.9 percent of the wholesalers and 9.8 percent of the agents in the country were located in New York in that year. The census of 1890 was the first to distinguish between wholesale and retail merchants but no breakdown by cities is furnished in the tables of occupations until the census of 1900 from which the above figures and those presented below for other centers are drawn.[2]

These wholesalers were not only numerous but were progressive in their business methods as well. The competition with other market centers provided an incentive for them to cultivate the New York wholesale trade area more extensively. At the same time, the competition among the jobbers in the city itself resulted in an intensive search for business within the existing trade area as well as an effort to secure new markets. Both these factors led to the same effect which was to strengthen the city's influence as a center of wholesale trade.

An illustration of the role of competition in enhancing and extending New York's position, and in altering methods of business operation, is contained in the following statement. It indicates also the high degree of development by 1880 in the boot and shoe trade:

> The jobbing branch of the business had a fair share of activity throughout the year, but the auction houses, which have hitherto been largely patronized complain of a falling off in their sales. The reason of this is, that the competiton between the jobbers is so great that the entire section from which the auctioneers derive their customers is so covered by drummers, that the retail dealers find that they can buy goods from sample at their own stores just as cheaply as they could get them by going to the trouble and expense of a trip to the city to attend the auction sales.[3]

The major factors upon which New York had built its preeminent position as a wholesale center were neatly summarized as early as 1876 in a report on the internal commerce of the country:

> The city of New York can rely for the maintenance of its commercial supremacy upon its enormous capital; the geographical advantages of its postiion as a distributing point; its direct connections with all parts of the United States by rail and water lines; the exclusive advantages of that important line of transportation formed by the lakes, the Erie Canal, and the Hudson River; the persistancy of its established commercial relations with almost every country on the globe; the energy and intelligence of its merchants, and the fact that it is the chief monetary center of the western continent.[4]

Chicago, second major center. During the latter half of the nineteenth century Chicago's development was so rapid that by the close of the period it occupied a position second only to that of New York as a center of wholesale trade. As early as 1867 the volume of sales in Chicago exceeded that in any other inland center and was surpassed only by the major seaport cities of New York, Philadelphia, Boston and New Orleans. Table IV shows the aggregate amount of business transacted in the twenty leading marketing centers during the fiscal year ending June 30, 1867. The figures include sales of wholesalers, auctioneers, merchandise brokers, and also retail dealers. To secure wholesale volume in absolute terms an estimate of the value of the latter category would have to be made and deducted from the total. Nevertheless, the figures are valid for comparison purposes without this refinement and show clearly the relative positions of the various cities as market centers in 1867.

TABLE IV

VOLUME OF BUSINESS TRANSACTED IN LEADING COMMERCIAL CITIES BY
WHOLESALE AND RETAIL DEALERS IN MERCHANDISE AND BY AUCTIONEERS
AND MERCHANDISE BROKERS, FISCAL YEAR ENDING JUNE 30, 1867

City	Volume of Business	Percent of Total
New York	$3,382,124,000	44.6
Boston	928,173,000	12.2
Philadelphia	662,097,000	8.8
New Orleans	526,795,000	7.0
Chicago	342,182,000	4.5
Baltimore	324,966,000	4.3
Cincinnati	213,253,000	2.8
St. Louis	213,034,000	2.8
San Francisco	151,367,000	2.0
Louisville	116,216,000	1.5
Milwaukee	110,675,000	1.5
Providence	91,876,000	1.2
Buffalo	81,350,000	1.1
Pittsburgh	80,939,000	1.1
Mobile	77,383,000	1.0
Brooklyn	69,676,000	.9
Detroit	62,757,000	.8
Cleveland	55,302,000	.7
Charleston	46,769,000	.6
Newark	36,428,000	.5
Total	$7,573,362,000	99.9

Source: Based on Report of the Special Commissioner of the Revenue,
House Executive Document No. 81, 40th Congress, 2nd Session,
January 7, 1868, p. 19.

The growth of Chicago appears to have been particularly
stimulated by the economic effects of the Civil War. The annual
reports of the trade and commerce of Chicago during and immediately
following the War emphasize the general prosperity enjoyed by the
city's business firms.[5] In addition, the War greatly impeded
business at St. Louis which was Chicago's closest competitor at the
time for the trade of the Mississippi valley and territories to the
west. Thus the Civil War hastened a process which had already been
started by the railroads, that of increasing the business of Chicago
and, at the same time, decreasing activity at St. Louis.[6]

Another major event, which had adverse effects for some of the
other centers but peculiarly enough worked to the ultimate benefit of
Chicago wholesalers, was the Panic of 1873. The western buyers who
had been in the habit of purchasing in the East because of the longer
credits available there found this source seriously curtailed by the
Panic. Consequently many of the western merchants began to
concentrate their business in Chicago since the wholesalers there
were in comparatively good financial condition. Chicago retained
much of this business in spite of later attempts by Eastern jobbers
to lure back their trade with renewed credit offerings and other
inducements. The buyers had found they could realize savings in
freight and other buying costs in Chicago which were not possible in
securing supplies from the eastern wholesale centers.[7]

Chicago's rise to the foremost position among the wholesale
centers in the midwest was further hastened by her transportation

advantages. The Lakes and the Erie Canal provided obvious advantages in communicating eastward. Aside from supplying a good natural waterway on which transportation was cheap, this route provided competition for the railroads serving Chicago. Consequently the city enjoyed advantages in the form of lower rail freight rates from the East than could be secured by some of the other competing midwestern centers.

The fact that the eastbound shipments from Chicago were bulky, grain, lumber, beef, and the like, and that the shipments westbound for Chicago were composed of less bulky manufactured articles resulted in a great deal of competition among the railroads for the traffic to Chicago from the East. This had the obvious advantage of reducing the cost of goods to Chicago wholesalers and making it possible for them to sell manufactured goods in Chicago, in some cases, almost as cheaply as they could be secured in the East. It also placed these merchants in a superior competitive position with respect to those in such centers as Louisville, Cincinnati, St. Louis, and other interior points.

The aggressiveness of Chicago businessmen in promoting their city as a wholesale center was also a factor in the rapid growth of that market. For example, St. Louis had early assumed a position of importance in the marketing structure of the Mississippi Valley. The capital there was largely controlled by bankers and a conservative mercantile element. These business leaders were apparently reluctant to supply risk capital, to promote the city as a good place to do business, and to make the innovations necessary to an expanding and progressive wholesale center.[8] This conservatism was probably instrumental in causing St. Louis to fall from the position of dominance as a wholesale trade center which it had formerly occupied.

The development of a trade center depends upon the competency of that center to meet the economic needs of the area tributary to it. Chicago had this competency by virture of its geographic situation, its position as a railroad hub, and the sagacity and aggressiveness of its merchants.

The area served by Chicago during this period of growth and development included practically the entire Northwest. Therein lies another reason for Chicago's rise to midwestern preeminence and its triumph over St. Louis as the center of trade in the Mississippi valley. The Southwest did not develop as rapidly or provide as rich a market or producing area as did the Northwest for which Chicago was the chief distributing point.

These, then, were the forces at work which helped to bring about a shift in the most important routes of internal trade from North-South to East-West and to foster the rise of Chicago as the western terminus for a large portion of that trade. Chicago had assumed its position of leadership by about 1875.[9]

The early importance of Chicago as a wholesale center is indicated by the extent of its trade area which, by 1880, included much of the northern and western United States:

It is evident from the foregoing facts,
that the trade of Chicago is not circumscribed
within sharply defined limits. The range of its
trade is world-wide, as is, or may be, that of
every other great commercial city. But in the
sense of being a primary market for the purchase
and sale of agricultural products of the western
and northerwestern States and Territories, and
for supplying general merchandise throughout
this region, the range of trade of Chicago
embraces, Illinois, Wisconsin, Northern
Michigan, Iowa, Northern Missouri, Kansas,
Nebraska, Colorado, the Territory of Dakota, the
Indian Territory, New Mexico, and the other
Territories as far west as the eastern borders
of the States of California and Oregon, an area
constituting more than one-half of the
territorial limits of the United States
exclusive of Alaska.[10]

Chicago, however, did not enjoy completely free and unlimited

access to this vast area with its rich markets. That there was

competition to be met is indicated by the following quotation which

also provides an idea of the trade areas of some of the other centers

which were among the major competitors of Chicago:

Within this entire area, however, the trade
of Chicago meets to a greater or less extent the
competition of the commercial enterprises of
other cities. The competition of Milwaukee is
met throughout Minnesota, Wisconsin, and
Northern Michigan; and the competition of Saint
Louis is met in Southern Iowa, Northern
Missouri, Southern Nebraska, the State of
Kansas, the Indian Territory, Colorado and New
Mexico. The Merchants of San Francisco, New
Orleans, and New York and other Atlantic
seaports, with respect to many lines of trade,
also compete directly throughout the entire
territory, within the ordinary trade limits of
Chicago.[11]

Wholesale houses operating in practically all the important

jobbing lines could be found in Chicago during this period. Those mentioned in the preceding chapter grew and flourished and many new

lines were added. In the dry goods trade, for example, the total

volume of sales for 1860 was estimated at $15,000,000.[12] By 1869

this trade had reached an annual volume of $33,000,000, in spite of a

price decline in that year of seven to eight percent. This business

was handled by eighteen wholesale houses.[13] In 1885 this trade

totaled more than $57,000,000. By that date the dry goods firms were

sending traveling salesmen as far as Oregon and Washington in the

northwest and California and Arizona in the southwest.[14]

Aside from the traditional jobbing lines of groceries, dry

goods, drugs, and hardware, Chicago did a considerable wholesale

trade in numerous lines. The following are wholesale volume figures

for some of these other lines of trade for the year 1887:[15]

Books...................	$12,500,000	Liquors........	$10,800,000
Carriages..............	2,000,000	Musical........	1,400,000
Coal...................	23,000,000	Organs.........	2,000,000
Crockery..............	5,000,000	Oysters........	2,300,000
Coal oil..............	6,000,000	Paper..........	21,000,000
Furs..................	1,800,000	Paper stock....	5,000,000
Fish..................	2,700,000	Pianos.........	2,500,000
Fruits................	3,000,000	Iron...........	15,000,000
Jewelry and Watches...	13,500,000	Woodenware.....	2,500,000
Leather goods.........	2,550,000	Wall Paper.....	1,275,000

The census returns for 1900 show that at that time there were

3,385 wholesale merchants and dealers in Chicago. It is probable

that their total volume of sales approximated $1,000,000,000. This

is based on an estimate for 1901 which places the aggregate wholesale

trade of Chicago in that year at $1,142,120,000.[16] The rapidity of

the development of Chicago as a center of trade is clearly indicated when we note that sales in 1860 were only about one-tenth as large as in 1900.[17] These differences would be even more striking if differences in prices were taken into consideration.[18]

Those, then, are some indications of the very rapid development of New York and Chicago as wholesale centers and the factors responsible for their growth during the period from 1860 to 1900. It should not be inferred from the discussion that the developments in these cities were the only ones taking place at this time which were important in shaping the future wholesale structure. The other major centers were continually expanding, although less rapidly than either New York or Chicago. In addition, by the last quarter of the century wholesale houses had been established in many of the smaller cities, a development which is worthwhile exploring.

Other Important Coastal Centers

For purposes of emphasis it seemed expedient to discuss the most important wholesale centers, New York and Chicago, first and independently. To avoid undue repetition, however, it seems equally desirable to consider Philadelphia, Boston, and Baltimore together. All three are coastal ports and many of the same factors were contributory to their growth. Each was secondary, as a wholesale marketing center, to New York although each experienced a rapid growth during the period and was important in its own right. Following the discussion of the growth of wholesaling in these three coastal cities attention will be directed to the wholesale markets, other than Chicago, which were important in the interior.

Philadelphia. Among the other leading wholesale centers at this time Philadelphia ranked high in importance in a number of lines in the trade area which it served.

Some of the more important of the lines handled by Philadelphia wholesalers by 1880 were boots and shoes, hardware, dry goods, produce, furniture, groceries, lumber, tobacco, drugs and so forth.[19] In a complete list practically all the jobbing lines would appear. Although Philadelphia was expanding it came nowhere near New York in the competitive race. Indeed, Philadelphia had difficulty in maintaining a constant relative position in the competition with New York. During this period it was simply a case of the continuance in operation of the forces mentioned above and in Chapter II, working in favor of New York. Given the conditions as they were the relegation of Philadelphia to second place was inevitable. The contemporary Philadelphians, nevertheless, were prone to blame this state of affairs on everything from unfair competition to deliberate discrimination by the railroads against Philadelphia.[20]

The rise of the wholesaling centers of the interior was not without its adverse competitive effects upon the seaboard markets. In Philadelphia complaints of this were common. In the case of the wholesale drug trade, for example, it was said in 1880 that, "The drifting away of the wholesale drug trade from the seaboard cities to the large trade centers of the West has gone on, and this with increased railroad facilities, is likely to continue."[21] The other

coastal cities, of course, faced the same competitive problem and

Philadelphia was not alone in feeling its effects.[22] New York,

however, probably felt this problem of competition from the interior

for wholesale trade less acutely than either Boston, Philadelphia, or

Baltimore because of the former's strong transportation ties with

Chicago. A great deal of trade flowed both ways between Chicago and

New York, an advantage which the other seaboard cities did not

have.

Indicative of the advancing state of development in wholesaling

in Philadelphia during this period is the number of agent and

merchant wholesalers then operative in the market. The Philadelphia

directory of 1887, for instance, lists the following: 41 general

merchandise brokers besides numerous ones specializing in such

commodities as drugs, cotton, coffee, grain, iron, lumber, wool, and

tobacco. In the clothing trade there were 51 wholesale merchants,

some of whom specialized in particular lines. In drugs there were 34

wholesale firms, 86 in groceries, and 26 in hardware. There were 136

general commission merchants besides those specializing by line and

those combining shipping and commission, importing and commission,

and forwarding operations.[23] The census data show that by 1900 there

were 1,209 individual wholesale merchants and dealers operating in

Philadelphia. Thus this market ranked third with reference to the

number of wholesalers, New York and Chicago having at that time 4,653

and 3,385 respectively.

Boston and Baltimore. Throughout the period both Boston and
Baltimore, the remaining two of the four major Atlantic ports,
developed rapidly as market centers and assumed positions of
importance in the wholesaling structure.

Statistical data pertaining to the volume of wholesale sales in
these two centers are not available for the latter decades of the
century. Table IV, however, shows their relative positions with
respect to volume of sales in the twenty leading cities in 1867. At
this time Boston occupied second place, exceeding Philadelphia, in
third place, by over 250 million; Baltimore, as shown, was sixth in
volume of sales. Although both cities made rapid strides, this
relationship was soon upset by the more rapid growth of New York and
Chicago.

Boston, although shortly being forced to relinquish its second
place position, nevertheless, continued to play a dominant role in
the trade of New England throughout the remainder of the century.[24]
In the early part of the period many of the New England textile mills
purchased southern cotton through Boston and, in turn, sold their
manufactured products via the same market. Ultimately, a good deal
of this trade was lost to Boston when these mills began dealing more
directly with their sources of supply and markets.

The boot and shoe industry, however, remained a lucrative trade
and was dominated by Boston through the close of the century. The
growth of this trade was very rapid. In 1871, for instance, Boston

shipped 1,254,223 cases of boots and shoes; in 1880 shipments reached 2,263,890 cases. The total for the decade was 15,915,581.[25]

It is apparent that Boston's growth was steady but less rapid than that of some of the other centers. There are several factors which account, at least in part, for this slower development.

Before 1860 Boston merchants had weathered the financial panics well. The Panic of 1873, however, proved to be a real setback and the volume of trade was reduced to a level approximately 12 percent below normal for the next five to six years.[26] Not until 1880, when the whole country entered into a period of prosperity, did Boston recoup its losses. The effects of the Panic probably would have been less severe as far as Boston merchants were concerned except that it came on the heels of the fire of 1872. This fire virtually wiped out the entire business district. The part of the city which was destroyed included the section where the wholesale dry goods, clothing, wool, shoe, leather, paper, and hardware firms were concentrated. The businesses destroyed were eventually rebuilt on a larger scale than ever but the fire and then the Panic were a severe setback.[27]

The railroads were responsible for the diversion of much of Boston's coastal trade to other centers. The rail rate differentials granted to Baltimore, Hampton Roads, Philadelphia, and Montreal on export-import traffic from and to the territory west of Buffalo and Pittsburgh were a handicap to Boston's development. In fairness to the other ports, however, it should be pointed out that the rail rate differential on export goods was approximately offset by the through rail and ocean rate differentials which were in Boston's favor.[28]

Baltimore occupied fourth place among the east coast seaports and wholesale centers. The competitive situation of Baltimore had been rather precarious up to the Civil War but it appears to have stabilized somewhat thereafter. The city's foreign commerce increased after the war and by 1867 domestic trade was growing, especially in cotton, naval stores, and other southern produce as well as in western grain and provisions.[29] Although Baltimore continued to grow absolutely it did not keep pace relatively with its rivals.

The major factors in the early growth of Baltimore were its location on the sea and and a hinterland rich in raw materials. The Baltimore and Ohio, reaching the Ohio river a year in advance of the Pennsylvania railroad, secured considerable trade for the city for a time. The extension of the Pennsylvania railroad to Baltimore, however, tended to make the city tributary to Philadelphia and New York and it eventually lagged behind in the railroad and harbor improvements races, all of which contributed to the decelerating rate of growth.[30]

The trade area of Baltimore was relatively restricted. The full potential of the Southern trade was not realized because of the

competition of other centers which were aggressively seeking to
expand at this time. The trade to the north and northwest was
largely usurped by centers in that area so that Baltimore's dominance
as a wholesale market seems to have been confined primarily to the
area to the near west and south. This, of course, is not meant to
imply that the city did no business elsewhere for it had extensive
lines of trade but actually dominated only a relatively small
sector.

Such were the developments among the four coastal centers, New
York, Philadelphia, Boston and Baltimore, and the great interior
market center, Chicago, during the last four decades of the
nineteenth century. Largely due to improvements in the general
economic environment they were all growing absolutely, some
relatively more than others.

Competition was keen but the competitive pie was large enough
to afford most of the wholesalers in these markets a comparatively
generous portion. They were not free, however, to divide it only
among themselves. The older centers in the interior also continued
to grow and numerous new ones were being established in the smaller
cities and towns.

Other Important Interior Centers

Cincinnati. Up to the time of the Civil War Cincinnati was the
leading commercial and wholesaling center of the interior. The
previous discussion has pointed out the reason for this as being

largely due to advantageous geographical location. Situated on a principal waterway Cincinnati was the major distributing center to the South and West for eastern manufactures and an assembly and purchasing point for western produce.

During the 1860's, however, both Chicago and St. Louis surpassed Cincinnati as centers of trade and population. The reason for this was given by one expert on internal trade as follows:

> The more rapid increase in the population of Chicago and Saint Louis is due mainly to the fact that they have become the principal primary markets for the surplus products of States and Territories west of the State of Ohio embracing about one-half of the territory of the United States, exclusive of Alaska, and to the fact that those cities have also become important commercial centers for the distribution of general merchandise in the States and Territories referred to.31

The most important competitor of Cincinnati after the Civil War, and the one which caused it the most concern, was Louisville. Previously Cincinnati had been the dominant figure in the southern commerce which it shared with Louisville and St. Louis. Now Louisville was seriously challenging its position as a leader in that trade. Furthermore, it was pointed out in 1881 that with the development of the railroads "the merchants of Boston, New York, Philadelphia, Baltimore and Chicago, and other towns and cities east and west, are able to carry on trade not only with the larger cities, but also with the smaller cities and towns in the Southern States. Besides, merchants and manufacturers now appear, through their agents, in every town and city of the South as buyers of the surplus product of that section."32

The Civil War halted the trade of Cincinnati with the southern states and after that time much of the western commerce shifted from the rivers to the railroads. This placed Cincinnati at a distinct disadvantage. In the first place improved rail transportation increased competition among the interior market centers and resulted in increased competition from the east. Secondly, Louisville was in a position to exploit Cincinnati's river commerce by charging exorbitant tolls for passage through the canal around the Ohio river falls at Louisville. This situation made it more difficult for Cincinnati river commerce to compete with that carried by rail. Finally, Cincinnati's volume declined because the city was slow in developing railroad transportation facilities.

The laws of the state at first prohibited any Ohio city from investing in or otherwise aiding private enterprise to build railroads and Cincinnati businessmen were apparently unwilling to promote them on their own. A special law was finally passed in 1869 which made it possible for the city to build and operate a railroad under a trusteeship. Thus it was that the Cincinnati Southern was opened in 1880 to traffic to Chattanooga where rail connections were available to all parts of the South. Although it had dominated southern trade on both sides of the Mississippi up to 1860, Cincinnati was the last of the four major cities of the west to tie into the southern railroad network by means of a railroad whose management was closely identified with its own commercial interests.

The completion of the Cincinnati Southern brought about a considerable decrease in freight rates between Cincinnati and the major southern markets. Cincinnati wholesalers were able to ship to the ports of the southern Atlantic and Gulf states and to interior points in North and South Carolina, Georgia, Alabama, and Mississippi at rates up to twenty percent less than had prevailed.[33] Other equally important advantages of the railroad to Cincinnati merchants was the fact that it supplied access to facilities for trade throughout the south and, secondly, that it prevented discrimination against Cincinnati by rival cities, particularly Louisville.

The opening of the Cincinnati Southern was a stimulus to Cincinnati trade but was not strong enough to help it regain the position of leadership it once held. An indication of the growth in the volume of the city's trade is contained in the following statement of the value of merchandise shipped from Cincinnati:[34]

```
1855 ......................... $ 38,777,394
1865 .........................   193,790,311
1875 .........................   201,404,023
1880 .........................   253,827,267
```

It is apparent that the trade of Cincinnati was growing absolutely throughout this period, especially considering the fact that the increases were attained in the face of a general decline in the level of wholesale prices.[35]

Relatively, however, St. Louis, Louisville, and Chicago were all outstripping Cincinnati and after 1880 growth of the latter was very slow. It is interesting to note the opinion of one authority who states that as far as metropolitan economy is concerned Cincinnati belongs to the past, that it has been surpassed by Cleveland which, in the same sense, belongs to the future. Metropolitan economy is here defined as existing in the large metropolis having a relatively large proportion of workers engaged in wholesaling with relatively few in manufacturing and showing little dependence on neighboring centers for trade and transport.[36] A further indication that the growth of Cincinnati, although steady, was slow during the latter part of the period is contained in the following excerpt from a work admittedly produced to point out the advantages of Cincinnati:

> Notwithstanding superior facilities for
> reaching the south, it is doubtful if there is
> any promise of extraordinary development in that
> direction, for this department of trade
> [groceries] shows rather a steady and wholesome
> growth, rather than any marked expansion.
> Cincinnati probably distributes the same
> quantity of goods, and there is little variation
> in scope taken for distribution as the years
> roll on.[37]

In the case of dry goods and clothing Cincinnati was in a somewhat better position. These were the leading trades of the city and their merchandise was distributed in most areas of the South and West.[38] Table V shows the volume in these and other leading lines for the last decade of the period and provides a further illustration

of the slow steady development. The hardware and drug trades are
conspicuous for their lack of attention in the annual trade reviews
of the Chamber of Commerce from which Table V was prepared.
Presumably the bulk of the early hardware trade carried on by
Cincinnati had been taken over by St. Louis and Chicago whose trade
in this line was flourishing.

Louisville. For many years Cincinnati's closest competitor was
Louisville. After 1860 Louisville developed rapidly at the expense
of Cincinnati, the former advancing while the latter grew at a
relatively slower rate. The principle reason for this was the
railroad monopoly possessed by Louisville. The Louisville and
Nashville railroad, which tapped the southern rail network, was
controlled and operated in the best interests of Louisville
merchants:

> The Cincinnati rail rates to and from local
> points on the Louisville and Nashville railroad
> were made by adding to the rates between
> Louisville and those points the rate between
> Cincinnati and Louisville. The rates between
> Cincinnati and competitive points were made by
> adding an arbitrary rate between Cincinnati and
> Louisville to the rate from Louisville to such
> points.[39]

The principal factor influencing the location of Louisville was
the falls in the Ohio river and this was also responsible for much of
the city's early growth during the era of water transportation. The
falls caused a stoppage at Louisville of the traffic moving in either
direction on the river and thus made the city an important forwarding

TABLE V

VOLUME OF SALES AT WHOLESALE IN
FOUR LEADING LINES OF TRADE,
CINCINNATI, 1890-1900

(In 000's of dollars)

Year	Boots & Shoes	Dry Goods	Clothing	Groceries
1889-90a	$11,027	$34,965	$21,060	$18,229
1890-91a	11,735	36,300	23,220	18,406
1891-92a	13,335	37,450	23,450	
1893	12,550	35,575	21,725	————b
1894	11,250	32,685	18,700	
1895	12,580	33,625	19,650	19,250
1896	11,350	31,475	18,875	17,500
1897	14,150	34,350	20,750	18,500
1898	15,500	34,500	21,250	19,600
1899	17,250	39,125	23,150	19,750
1900	19,325	37,150	25,575	20,725

aFiscal years.

bThese data not available.

Source: Cincinnati Chamber of Commerce, Annual Reports, 1890-1900.

and distributing point. Most important, perhaps, in its continued
growth was the fact that Louisville maintained and even increased
this advantage during the early days of the era of railroad
construction.

By 1880 Louisville had experienced a considerable growth and
was supplying a large wholesale trade area. Also by this time the
wholesalers of Louisville were beginning to feel the effects of the
competition of some of the other trade centers with which the
railroads were bringing them into close contact. It was said of the
grocery trade in 1880, for example, that "The volume of trade in
Louisville in staple groceries and provisions has largely increased
during the era of railway transportation, although the area of this
trade as a whole is more circumscribed and competition is much
greater."[40] By this time there were a large number of wholesale
grocery merchants in Louisville whereas twenty years earlier there
had been only three or four.

The trend in the dry goods trade was exactly opposite to that
in groceries. Where before the Civil War there had been a
considerable number of dry goods wholesalers in Louisville there were
only five in 1880. These five, however, handled a business 100 per
cent greater than previously, the volume having increased from three
to six million dollars.[41] Although this point will be discussed in
detail in the next chapter, it is interesting to note the
illustration provided here by the grocery and dry goods trades in

Louisville at this time. Both operating out of the same city with
the same facilities, both trades handling a class of products with
similar characteristics yet the former tending toward a large number
of smaller firms and the latter toward a small number of large firms.
The answer to this presumably lies in differing margin-cost
relationships and market considerations for the two trades.

That the trade area of Louisville was extensive is shown by the
following:

> The area of trade in this line of goods
> which Louisville enters and partially supplies
> dry goods has always been larger than her
> distribution for groceries. It extends further
> south, southeast, and southwest, entering even
> the cities of Mobile, New Orleans, and
> Galveston, and all the Southern States west of
> Georgia, and including the northern part of the
> state. Competition is very heavy and just after
> the war the business paid the heaviest profits.
> Louisville has very little trade in this line
> North of the Ohio river, whilest south of that
> stream she is thrown into competition with New
> York, Baltimore, Philadelphia, Cincinnati, St.
> Louis, and Chicago, and in more limited
> territories, Nashville, Memphis, and the more
> important southern distributing centers, to all
> of which she sends some merchandise of this kind
> herself.[42]

The competition mentioned in the preceding quotation became
more and more severe for Louisville. Again, as was the case with
Cincinnati and some of the eastern centers, it must be noted that the
relative growth of Louisville ultimately slowed down, especially in
the latter part of the period. The railroad monopoly was eventually
destroyed by new rail construction such as the Cincinnati Southern

and with it the absolute advantage of Louisville over some of the other wholesale centers.[43]

St. Louis. The basis of the early commercial growth of St. Louis was its location at the heart of the most important system of internal waterways and the development of the steamboat. This fact alone would seem to account largely for the difficulties St. Louis faced in adjusting to the economic changes brought about by the railroads. The merchants in the city did not comprehend the full significance of this development until it was nearly too late, until a large portion of their trade area had been permanently taken over by Chicago.[44]

Within a few years after the Civil War Chicago's dominance in the North and Northwest had become apparent and St. Louis was forced to turn to the West, South and Southwest to develop its trade.[45] It was primarily because the latter section developed more slowly than the Northwest that St. Louis lost in the struggle for commercial dominance in the Mississippi valley.[46] The total value of the wholesale business at St. Louis for 1869 was estimated at $195,000,000 while that of Chicago was estimated to be $400,000,000 in 1869.[47]

St. Louis was suffering in the competitive race with Chicago but it was doing very well in other directions. The wholesale trade interests of St. Louis and New Orleans, for example, had for years been complementary. The railroads reversed that situation:

> The Missouri, Kansas and Texas and the Iron
> Mountain Railroads have given Saint Louis an
> opportunity of forcing her trade upon Texas,
> though she is much further off than New Orleans.
> She is not only putting groceries, dry goods,
> drugs, shoes, hats, and millinery goods, all
> brought from the East by rail into Texas, but
> she is drawing away the grain and cotton. These
> articles are, for want of Railroads to New
> Orleans, taken to St. Louis, nearly double the
> distance it is to New Orleans, not because Saint
> Louis is a good market for them, for she is not,
> especially for cotton, but simply because Saint
> Louis has had the enterprise to build railroads
> and push a trade in Texas. She acts as
> trade-carrier, banker, broker, forwarding and
> commission merchant, and is compelled to take
> Texas products in payment for what she imports,
> forwards, and sells there.[48]

The opinion set forth in the preceding statement regarding the

relative merits of New Orleans and St. Louis as grain markets is of

questionable accuracy for St. Louis had, by this time, a considerable

direct trade with eastern and also European ports in grain and cereal

products. The pertinent part of the quotation concerning the

extension of the St. Louis trade area into Texas, however, is

undoubtedly correct coming as it does not as an indiscriminate claim

by St. Louis but as a bitter admission of defeat from New Orleans.

The trade area of St. Louis in 1880 can be defined

approximately as follows. The St. Louis merchants dominated the

southern and central portion of Missouri, all of Arkansas, most of

Texas and the northwest portion of Louisiana. Although sales were

made west of the Mississippi and north of the Missouri they were

relatively insignificant because of the competition of Chicago in that area. In northern Missouri, Kansas, and southern Nebraska the trade was shared by St. Louis and Chicago both competing vigorously for the overland trade with the Pacific coast states. East of the Mississippi and north of the Ohio, St. Louis was definitely limited by the competition of the eastern centers although it did dominate a considerable portion of the trade in parts of southern Illinois, Indiana, and Ohio. To the southeast competition was also strong and St. Louis' trade was relatively static in that section.[49] These areas are delimited in the sense of St. Louis being the principal market for the sale of general merchandise and for the purchase of surplus agricultural products from those areas.

Data are not available with which to circumscribe the trade area in 1900. Reference is made in the contemporary literature, however, to an area "known as St. Louis territory" which lay to the south and southwest. In the case of dry goods, the largest of the jobbing lines in terms of volume, daily and weekly shipments were being made to Alabama, Arizona, Arkansas, California, Colorado, Florida, Louisiana, Michigan, Missouri, Montana, Nebraska, New Mexico, Texas, and some to the far Northwest. The wholesale trade in hardware was concentrated primarily south and southwest of the city.[50]

Table VI presents the volume in certain lines of wholesale trade for 1900 and for 1890 to the extent that the latter are available. These data provide an interesting contrast to those for 1860 presented in Chapter II.

TABLE VI

VOLUME OF SALES AT WHOLESALE IN SELECTED
LINES OF TRADE IN ST. LOUIS
FOR 1890 and 1900[a]

Item	Volume of Sales	
	1890	1900
Dry goods	$35,000,000	$80,000,000
Groceries	73,000,000	70,000,000
Boots and shoes	21,000,000[b]	37,500,000
Tobacco and cigars		40,000,000
Hardware	14,000,000	31,500,000
Woodenware		8,500,000
Lumber		13,500,000
Candies		3,750,000
Clothing		3,500,000
Furniture		36,000,000
Paints and paint oils		6,000,000
Hats, caps and gloves	3,000,000	4,500,000
Drugs and kindred items		35,000,000
Glass and glassware		5,500,000

[a]Current prices.

[b]Includes wholesale sales by manufacturers of $7,000,000.

Source: St. Louis Merchants' Exchange, Annual Reports, 1890, 1900.

Smaller Cities as Wholesale Centers

The foregoing includes the largest of the leading wholesale centers which developed during the period under consideration. These do not, however, by any means include all of the wholesalers or account for all of the wholesaling done during that time. There were a number of smaller cities whose wholesale operations were comparatively extensive and who were in competition with the centers discussed above. In addition to these there were still other wholesalers in the smaller towns many of which developed as secondary centers within the wholesale trade area of such cities as New York, Chicago, and St. Louis.

Kansas City. Representative, from a wholesaling point of view, of this intermediate or secondary class of wholesale marketing centers was Kansas City. The early growth of this city was largely due to its natural advantages in transportation. Located at the junction of the Kansas and Missouri rivers it had access to water transport facilities and the country to the west was well suited to overland travel. The railroads largely followed the natural route of trade so that Kansas City early became an important rail center and its transportation advantages were thus extended.

At the close of the Civil War Kansas City appeared to have been overcome by Leavenworth in the race for commercial supremacy. Leavenworth was then a city of some 15,000 population and controlled the trade in Southern Kansas and in parts of New Mexico and

Colorado.[51] It is interesting to note in passing that Leavenworth is
the oldest grocery jobbing point in Kansas, a wholesale grocery house
having been established there in 1858.[52]

By the close of 1870, however, Kansas City had surpassed
Leavenworth and had achieved, primarily on the basis of
transportation advantages, an important position as a center of
wholesale trade. The volume of trade for that year was estimated at
about $2,511,000 in dry goods, $2,614,000 in groceries, liquors
$518,000, and $3,000,000 in all other lines for a total wholesale
volume of $8,000,000. The aggregate business of the city for the
year was estimated to have exceeded $34,000,000.[53]

The growth of Kansas City was extremely rapid, its population
increasing from 5,000 in 1865 to 67,977 in 1880. This growth was
based largely on trade since manufacturing was not yet well
established.[54] The wholesale trade in the latter year included a
wide area:

> The territorial limits of the jobbing trade
> of Kansas City may, in general terms, be said to
> be Kansas, Colorado, New Mexico, Texas, and the
> western half of Missouri, the southwestern
> quarter of Iowa, and the southern half of
> Nebraska. The dry goods trade covers all this
> territory; the grocery trade all; the provision
> trade all south and west; the agricultural
> implement trade covers all except parts of
> Colorado and New Mexico, which are not
> agricultural, and others.[55]

By 1890 Kansas City had become an important wholesale center
competing successfully in its trade area with the larger of the firms

from New York, Chicago and St. Louis. Sales were made in every state
and territory west of the Mississippi and even into some of the
southeastern states. The trade areas for agricultural implements,
dry goods and groceries were especially large.[56]

Table VII is a summary of the jobbing trade in Kansas City for
the year ending June 30, 1891. The data are interesting as an
indicator of the nature of the trade at that time and also because it
is unusual to find such detailed information available on any of the
centers before the first census of distribution. The table shows
that there was over $97,000,000 worth of merchandise distributed by
the jobbers of Kansas City in 60 different lines of trade. This
statement, of course, does not include livestock and grain in which
trades Kansas City was among the leaders in 1890. The volume of
wholesale sales at this time shows an increase of more than 1,000
percent over 1870, the earliest year for which an estimate of the
total is available. By 1900 there were over 700[b] wholesale merchants
and dealers in Kansas City.

Minneapolis and St. Paul. Another center which developed
rapidly during this period, and which is illustrative of about the
same class as Kansas City in terms of wholesaling, is Minneapolis-
St. Paul. These are the so-called "twin cities" of the northwest.
They have been, for all practical purposes, a single economic unit
since about 1880 and should be so considered. Nevertheless, their
early growth as wholesale centers was more or less distinct and that

TABLE VII

WHOLESALE TRADE OF KANSAS CITY FOR THE YEAR ENDING JUNE 30, 1891

Class	No.	Capital	Stock	Sales	Employees
Agric. implements	29	$1,587,500	$1,372,500	$7,755,000	494
Beer	7	526,000	133,025	1,239,000	93
Boots & shoes	5	215,000	430,000	1,725,500	72
Builders iron	5	10,000	28,500	100,400	9
Carriages	5	212,000	163,500	645,000	31
Cigars & tobacco	23	434,500	366,600	1,596,000	55
Coal	22	702,500	59,050	3,287,062	513
Coffees,teas, spices	7	557,500	118,000	2,230,000	75
Clothing	6	242,000	174,500	1,045,000	21
Crockery	3	78,000	225,500	535,000	65
Drugs	7	630,500	498,500	2,323,000	121
Dry goods & millinery	7	1,107,000	1,135,000	4,265,000	251
Elec. supplies	5	46,500	48,000	186,700	19
Fish and oysters	6	76,500	12,100	580,000	59
Flour	6	75,000	49,500	1,220,743	48
Furn. & carpet	6	606,000	440,000	1,738,000	171
Fruit & produce	59	438,800	222,050	5,623,242	286
Gravel & sand	7	76,000	15,200	922,000	58
Groceries	22	1,792,500	831,500	21,332,000	324
Hardware	4	755,000	825,000	2,400,000	178
Hats & furnishings	6	180,000	223,000	855,000	21
Hay & feed	20	119,000	70,300	3,116,500	82
Hides,wool,tallow	5	690,000	662,000	3,245,000	234
Ice	5	130,000	56,000	292,000	120
Jewelry	7	150,000	101,000	505,000	30
Leather	4	26,700	36,000	155,000	12
Lime, cement, plaster	4	195,000	38,000	475,000	92
Liquors	35	1,210,000	1,374,500	4,485,469	300
Lumber	31	2,200,000	842,500	8,987,000	602
Machinery	10	310,000	88,500	493,250	59
Mantels,grates	3	52,400	26,000	75,000	20
Marble tile	3	7,000	24,000	271,000	23
Mdse. brokers	6	30,000	1,000	4,950,000	17

(cont'd. on next page)

TABLE VII, cont'd.

WHOLESALE TRADE OF KANSAS CITY FOR THE YEAR ENDING JUNE 30, 1891

Class	No.	Capital	Stock	Sales	Employees
Metals	3	100,000	55,000	406,691	35
Notions	3	156,500	125,800	420,000	35
Nurseries	3	21,000	63,000	67,000	60
Paints,glass & oil	8	270,000	189,000	1,050,000	98
Paper	4	173,500	209,500	940,000	65
Railroad & bridge mat.	3	43,000		695,000	52
Sewing machines	5	124,500	70,000	337,200	121
Seeds	3	55,000	46,000	85,000	
Stationery and books	14	250,000	254,200	959,000	189
Vinegar, pickles	4	57,000	57,000	375,000	30
Windmills, plumbing	5	320,000	320,000	1,005,000	49
Woolens	4	88,500	88,500	282,000	10
Miscellaneous*	18	445,000	340,000	3,436,750	155
Total	457	$17,530,100	$12,397,825	$97,862,707	5,454

Source: Drawn from the Kansas City Board of Trade, Twelfth Annual Report, pp. 61-62.

*These include chemicals, sales, billiard tables and supplies, photographic supplies, rubber goods, engineers' instruments, stoves, advertising novelties, ventilating machinery, physicians' supplies, woodenware, musical instruments, sporting goods, and type.

of Minneapolis the more striking. Because of this, and because
Minneapolis has become the more prominent, it perhaps receives more
emphasis in the present discussion. Since many of the factors behind
the wholesale developments in the two cities are the same and because
the pertinent data are reported separately, to treat each in equal
detail would only result in unnecessary repetition and undue length.

The reasons for the selection of the geographical sites for the
two cities are obvious, the major one being the falls in the
Mississippi river. More important to the present discussion,
however, are the reasons for their growth and development as
wholesale centers. St. Paul was located on the Mississippi and had
become a center of trade by the time Minneapolis was established.
Eastern merchants sought to gain a share in the wholesale trade of
the northwest and established branches at St. Paul well before the
Civil War.[57] The fur trade was also a definite factor in the early
growth of the town. By 1857 St. Paul retailers had become large
enough that they were also supplying goods to country merchants in
the surrounding territory and thus developed a wholesale trade with
other towns.[58] It was not until the decade of the sixties, however,
that firms were established in St. Paul which sold exclusively at
wholesale.[59]

After 1860 the city's development was quickened due largely to
the rapid rate at which the surrounding areas were being settled and
developed and to the ultimate establishment of rail connections with

the east. By 1869 St. Paul claimed 62 wholesale houses doing a total
volume of over $8,000,000. Sales in three lines, groceries, dry
goods, and wool, furs, and hides were said to have exceeded one
million dollars each. The following are approximate figures of
wholesale volume in St. Paul for selected years up to 1900:[60]

1872	$ 17,500,000
1877	27,800,000
1881	46,500,000
1883	67,900,000
1889	109,000,000
1900	200,000,000

The early development of Minneapolis was centered on
manufacturing rather than distributive industries. This was due
primarily to the fact that St. Paul was already established as a
wholesale center and because Minneapolis was advantageously located
for manufacturing using the Falls in the Mississippi as a source of
power. Nevertheless, although it got a later start, the wholesale
trade of Minneapolis grew equally as rapidly as that of St. Paul and
had surpassed the latter by 1890.

The absolute growth of Minneapolis trade was due to the
influence of the same factors which were responsible for the
development of St. Paul, the major one of these being the rapid
growth and development of the Northwest. The next problem then is to
explain why Minneapolis was able to outstrip its twin in the race for
wholesale trade. The answer appears to lie in the fact that
Minneapolis' mills and elevators made it the chief market for grain,
the foremost product of the Northwest, and the trade of the area

followed to the same market.[61] Another contributing factor was the
specialization in jobbing lines which took place between the two
cities; Minneapolis early developed a relatively large trade in
agricultural implements, machinery and hardware. The trade area
being largely agricultural obviously supplied a fertile market for
these items.

The fact that Minneapolis' development was somewhat later, but
even more rapid, than that of St. Paul is illustrated in the
following figures of wholesale trade:[62]

1876	$ 5,373,000
1877	8,147,000
1878	10,406,000
1879	14,001,000
1880	24,299,000
1881	33,136,000
1882	37,518,000
1883	48,138,000
1884	58,627,500
1885	61,082,200
1886	68,950,000
1887	73,584,000

In 1870 there were only two or three firms engaged in selling
goods exclusively at wholesale and the total trade that year probably
did not exceed one million dollars.[63] Practically all of the early
wholesale houses in Minneapolis were outgrowths of expanding retail
firms. The first exclusively wholesale drug house was not
established until 1869.[64] It was some years later before similar
houses were opened in other lines. By 1892, however, Minneapolis was
well established as a wholesale center. It had surpassed St. Paul in
terms of volume and was a serious contender for some of the markets

claimed by Chicago and St. Louis. A summary of the trade for that
year and the preceding one is shown in Table VIII. In 1900 this
trade amounted to over $200,000,000 which would indicate that the
twin cities were about equal in terms of purely distributive trade.[65]
But when the $110,943,043 worth of sales of manufactures produced
and sold at wholesale in Minneapolis are added it is clearly the
leader.

Milwaukee. It will be interesting to note briefly the rise of
wholesaling in one last center belonging more or less in the same
class as Kansas City and the Twin cities, that is Milwaukee. This
city got off to an earlier start in wholesaling than either of the
other two but before 1900 had been outdistanced by them. Its
evolution was much like that of Minneapolis. Trade began first in
furs and proceeded into general merchandise with a retail center
developing. The retailers gradually enlarged the scope of their
operations to include some jobbing and finally there emerged the
exclusively wholesale firms handling a rather extended line. The
final step was the establishment of firms selling a specialized line
at wholesale only. This is a pattern which is apparent in the
development of practically all these centers.

The principal factor in Milwaukee's early growth was its
geographic location providing access to navigation and trade on the
Great Lakes. Moreover, its trade area to the west included a rich
agricultural area which developed steadily providing fertile markets.

TABLE VIII

VOLUME OF SALES AT WHOLESALE BY LINES OF TRADE
MINNEAPOLIS, 1891-92

Trade	1891	1892
Groceries, spices	$12,000,000	$15,000,000
Agricultural implements	7,200,000	10,000,000
Fruit, produce, fish	10,100,000	12,000,000
Lumber, lath, shingles	6,500,000	8,250,000
Hardware and stoves	5,400,000	6,210,000
Boots, shoes, rubber goods	3,106,000	3,490,000
Meat, hides, wood, coal	6,000,000	6,600,000
Dry goods, hats, caps	6,300,000	7,575,000
Cigars and liquor	3,103,000	3,400,000
Seeds	315,000	390,000
Furniture	1,204,000	1,370,000
Harness, leather, findings	575,000	630,000
Paper, stationery	1,500,000	2,000,000
Jewelry, crockery	357,000	975,000
Building material	1,400,000	1,900,000
Mill supplies	575,000	690,000
Shirts and furnishings	370,000	425,000
Flour output jobbed	37,170,490	42,632,600
Drugs, glass and misc.	4,100,000	7,750,000
Total	$107,275,490	$131,287,600

Source: Minneapolis Chamber of Commerce, Tenth Annual Report
(Minneapolis, 1892), p. 301.

It was estimated in 1856 that the trade area included nearly 500,000 people and that the railroads completed during that year would provide access to as many more which should shortly double the volume of wholesale trade.[66] These great expectations, although apparently well-founded at the time, were not realized because of the encroachments of Chicago, Minneapolis and St. Paul upon the trade area of Milwaukee. Chicago particularly became a strong rival.

As early as 1856 there were twenty wholesale grocery houses in the city along with eight in dry goods. In all, the wholesale volume amounted to $17,000,000. Two firms had sales of over $500,000, three sold over $400,000, and eight exceeded $300,000.[67] In spite of severe competition Milwaukee continued to grow. The wholesale trade for 1873 was $46,799,240; in 1895 it reached $98,305,000 having more than doubled in a little over two decades.[68]

Summary

Such was the growth of the centers from which the wholesale trade of the country was largely controlled from 1860 to 1900. There were numerous factors accounting for the rapid development of these centers in absolute terms. These factors might best be summarized under the heading of general economic growth and expansion. There were also specific factors accounting for the relative rate of growth of the several centers. The major development took place first in the cities whose location afforded the greatest advantage in transportation. Thus the seaboard centers were the first to gain preeminence in wholesaling, followed closely by the interior cities located on inland waterways such as Cincinnati, Chicago, and St. Louis. Then followed the establishment of still other jobbing points located, in some cases, at points other than along waterways.

The railroad fostered the growth of these newer centers but it also tended to strengthen the absolute, if not the relative, position of most of the older established marketing centers. New York, for example, extended its supremacy in waterway transport into the railroad era becoming a major terminus for the east-west lines running from Chicago.

Toward the end of the period, with the completion of the railroad network and the adjustment of rates, another factor assumed some importance in the relative progress of the wholesale centers. This was a factor which was sometimes overlooked but was nonetheless important, that is, the intelligence, aggressiveness, and business acumen of the wholesale merchants in the center. This applies, of course, collectively as well as individually. It was the activities of boards of trade, chambers of commerce and other local merchant and business organizations which were often instrumental in influencing improvements in harbors, railroad routes and rates, and advertising the advantages of a particular center throughout its potential trade area.

The pattern of growth was obviously largely similar for the centers within each class. Even though each city was in a different phase of development at any particular time they all went through the various phases at one time or another. Actually the differences were mainly those of degree. Broadly speaking there was first the establishment of a general trade. This was followed by specialization by function and by lines of trade and, finally, expansion in numbers of lines and volume in each line, leading to the attainment of full status as a center of wholesale trade.

FOOTNOTES - CHAPTER III

[1]Annual Reports, New York Chamber of Commerce.

*Domestic merchandise only.

**The figures pertaining to agents must, of course, be interpreted carefully since types other than agent wholesalers are included in these data. Nevertheless, the percentages are valid for comparison purposes since the number of agents other than wholesale middlemen would seem to be about the same in all the major centers.

[2]United States Twelfth Census, 1900, Occupations at the Twelfth Census, pp. 427-763.

[3]New York Chamber of Commerce, Twenty-Third Annual Report, 1880-81, Part II, p. 60.

[4]Annual Report of the Chief of the Bureau of Statistics, 1876, Part II, First Annual Report of the Internal Commerce of the United States (Washington, 1877), p. 85.

[5]See, for example, Annual Review of the Trade, Business and Growth of Chicago and the Northwest (Chicago, 1865).

[6]W.W. Belcher, The Economic Rivalry Between St. Louis and Chicago 1850-1880 (New York: Columbia University Press, 1947), p. 139.

[7]J. Moses and J. Kirkland, The History of Chicago (Chicago: Munsell and Company, 1895), p. 289.

[8]Belcher, op. cit., pp. 115-6.

[9]Report on the Internal Commerce of the United States, 1880, Chief of the Bureau of Statistics, Treasury Department (Washington, 1881), p. 101.

[10]Ibid., p. 105.

[11]Loc. cit.

[12]Chicago Board of Trade, Third Annual Statement of the Trade and Commerce of Chicago for Year Ending December 31st, 1860 (Chicago, 1861), p. 56.

[13]Moses and Kirkland, op. cit., p. 289.

[14]Ibid., p. 290.

[15]Commercial and Architectural Chicago (Chicago: G.W. Greer, 1887), p. 193.

[16]Dun's Review, January 8, 1910, p. 85.

[17]See Chapter II, page 23.

[18]Although it is not strictly within the scope of this study it is interesting to note some figures of Chicago's subsequent growth. It was not until 1927 that there were any detailed census data available. In that year a census of distribution was conducted in Chicago by the United States Bureau of the Census covering wholesale and retail trade for 1926. It was published by the Chicago Chamber of Commerce under the title Wholesale and Retail Trade of Chicago, Illinois. The summary of returns from this census is presented below. The data are of interest because they illustrate the continuing growth of the center and because they are among the first of the data of this type to become available.

> Number of establishments 7,297
> Number of employees 122,181
> Firm members and proprietors   4,744
> Total persons engaged 126,555
> Salaries and wages of employees $258,068,800
>   (Exclusive of compensation of props.)
> Average inventory at cost 281,411,400
> Sales $4,844,761,000

[19]Philadelphia Board of Trade, Forty-Seventh Annual Report (Philadelphia, 1880), pp. 112-9.

[20]F.S. Gowen, The Railway Problem (Philadelphia, 1881).

[21]Philadelphia Board of Trade, Forty-Seventh Annual Report (Philadelphia, 1880), p. 115.

[22]Annual Report of the Chief of the Bureau of Statistics, Commerce and Navigation, 1876, Internal Commerce of the United States, Part II, pp. 100-1.

[23]Gopsill's Philadelphia Business Directory for 1887.

[24]Boston Tercentenary Committee, Subcommittee on Memorial History, Fifty Years of Boston (Boston, 1932), p. 182.

[25]Boston Board of Trade, Twenty-Seventh Annual Report (Boston, 1881), p. 115.

[26]Boston Tercentenary Committee, op. cit., p. 180.

[27]Ibid., p. 179 and Boston Illustrated (Boston, 1878), pp. 8, 56.

[28]Boston Tercentenary Committee, op. cit., pp. 159-60.

[29]Board of Trade of Baltimore, Eighteenth Annual Report (Baltimore, 1868), p. 4.

[30]N.S.B. Gras, An Introduction to Economic History (New York: Harper's, 1922), p. 293.

[31]Joseph Nimmo, Jr., Report on the Internal Commerce of the United States, 1880 (Washington, 1881), p. 74.

[32]Ibid., p. 78.

[33]Ibid., pp. 94-5.

[34]Ibid., p. 75.

[35]See chart page 62.

[36]Gras, op. cit., pp. 293-4.

[37]Andrew Morrison, The Industries of Cincinnati (Cincinnati, 1886), p. 94.

[38]Cincinnati Chamber of Commerce, Thirty-Third Annual Report (Cincinnati, 1881), p. 117.

[39]Nimmo, op. cit., p. 90.

[40]C.H. Pope, "Statement in Regard to the Trade Areas of Louisville, Kentucky with some Considerations Relative to the Manufacturing and Distributive Interests of that City, 1880," in J. Nimmo, Report on the Internal Commerce of the United States, 1881 (Washington, 1881), Appendix No. 61, p. 127.

[41]Ibid., p. 80.

[42]Loc. cit.

[43]A.E. Parkins, The South, Its Economic-Geographic Development (New York: John Wiley and Sons, Inc., 1938), p. 474.

[44]Belcher, op. cit., p. 72.

[45]George H. Morgan, "Answers to Inquiries in Relation to the Commerce of Saint Louis, and the Commercial Movements to and from that City," in J. Nimmo, First Annual Report on the Internal Commerce of the United States, 1876 (Washington, 1876), Appendix No. 13, p. 157.

[46]Ibid., p. 180.

[47]Chicago Tribune, Annual Review of the Trade and Commerce of Chicago for the Year Ending December 31, 1869, p. 101. (Although these estimates were made by a Chicago newspaper there is no particular reason to question their validity, but even allowing for possible bias the difference is still striking.)

[48]New Orleans Times, January 6, 1877. Quoted in First Annual Report on Internal Commerce of the United States, 1876 (Washington, 1877), p. 109.

[49]J. Nimmo, Report on the Internal Commerce of the United States, 1881 (Washington, 1881), p. 126.

[50]St. Louis Merchant's Exchange, Annual Statement of the Trade and Commerce of St. Louis, 1900 (St. Louis, 1901), pp. 33, 40.

[51]C.W. Whitney, History of Kansas City, Missouri (Chicago: S.J. Clarke, 1908), p. 204.

[52]W.G. Hutchinson, "Decentralization in Grocery Jobbing," Kansas Studies in Business No. 5, Bureau of Business Research, University of Kansas, 1926, p. 41.

[53]W.H. Miller, The History of Kansas City (Kansas City, 1881), p. 129.

[54]Kansas City Board of Trade, Fourth Annual Report (Kansas City, 1881), p. 16.

[55]J. Nimmo, Report on the Internal Commerce of the United States (Washington, 1881), Appendix 28, p. 217.

[56]Kansas City Board of Trade, Twelfth Annual Report (Kansas City, 1891), pp. 63-74.

bIncluding 47 located in Kansas City, Kansas.

57M.D. Shutter, ed., History of Minneapolis (Chicago, 1923),
  p. 316.

58Gras, op. cit., p. 300.

59M.L. Hartsough, "The Twin Cities as a Metropolitan Market,"
  Minnesota University Studies in the Social Sciences, No. 18, 1925,
  p. 33.

60Ibid., pp. 34, 52.

61Shutter, op. cit., p. 316.

62Minneapolis Chamber of Commerce, Tenth Annual Report, 1892, p. 302.
  It should be noted that since these figures do not include grain
  and lumber they are not strictly comparable with the data presented
  for St. Paul.

63Op. cit., 1883, p. 102.

64Shutter, op. cit., p. 319.

65Ibid., p. 323. Hartsough, op. cit., p. 52.

66W.G. Bruce, ed., History of Milwaukee (Chicago, 1922), Vol. I, p.
  265.

67Loc. cit.

68Milwaukee Chamber of Commerce, Annual Reports.

CHAPTER IV

THE DEVELOPMENT OF THE WHOLESALE MERCHANT, 1860-1900

With the rise of the wholesale centers during the latter half of the nineteenth century came equally far-reaching developments on the part of wholesale merchants in the United States. This was a formative period for these middlemen and one in which many fundamental changes and innovations were made in the method and scope of their operations. It is the purpose of the present chapter to examine and clarify these phenomena in terms of the reasons for their occurrence and their effect upon the wholesale merchant and his methods of doing business.

Specialization by Wholesale Merchants

The trend toward specialization by wholesale merchants was clearly discernible in 1860. In the following forty years this tendency continued at an accelerated rate due primarily to the continually increasing size of the market. Moreover, this movement took more than one direction. First, there was a very noticeable increase in the number of wholesale merchants specializing by function, that is, selling at wholesale only. Secondly, there was an increase in the number specializing by lines of goods. Thirdly, there was not only an increase in the number of these wholesale firms specializing by lines of goods but there was an increase in the number of lines in which they operated.

Functional specialization. Foremost among these trends was
that toward specialization by function. The first step in this
development, the separation of wholesale and retail operations,
became especially noticeable after the Civil War and was largely
completed by the end of the nineteenth century. Closely following
was the movement toward separation of agent and merchant wholesaler
operations. As indicated in Chapter II it was not unusual in 1860 to
find the wholesale merchant performing one or even several types of
agent middlemen's functions. By 1900 this was the exception rather
than the rule.

During this time the separation of wholesaling from importing
was completed and the jobber disappeared as a separate intermediary.
It had formerly been the practice for jobbers to buy from importers
to sell to retailers or, in some cases, to other wholesale middlemen.
In this and the next two paragraphs the term jobber is used as it was
defined in 1860. Then it referred to a wholesale middleman who
bought from importers and made up assortments for sale to retailers
and other middlemen in smaller quantities. Subsequently, the term
was applied, in some trades, to those who sold in "job lots" or very
small quantities. It sometimes refers to a small middleman between
the wholesale merchant and the retailer. In other lines it is used
synonymously with merchant wholesaler.[1] The economic justification
for the jobber's existence lay in his performance of a necessary
function. He broke bales and packages into smaller lots and made up

assortments for sale to the retailers. A common channel for imported goods was, therefore, importer-jobber-retailer-consumer.[2]

In 1860 the wholesale merchant was defined as "a dealer who buys first hand, from manufacturer or importer, and who does not 'break the original bulk' of articles he deals in, for instance, selling not less than a cask of tallow, a butt or hogshead of wine, a chest of tea, or a bale of hides."[3] This was undoubtedly a sound description of the early wholesale merchant strictly defined. After 1860, however, wholesale merchants began to buy from importers or manufacturers and to sell to retailers often without the intervention of the jobber or any other middleman at any stage in the distribution channel. The functions of the jobber were being absorbed and thus in some lines the terms jobber and wholesale merchant came to mean generally the same type of organization.

There were several reasons for the disappearance of the jobber and the shifting of functions. The typical channel became that of manufacturer-wholesale merchant-retailer-consumer, partly because of the efforts of those in each stage to bring themselves into closer contact with the succeeding stages in the trade channel. The importer invaded the field of the jobber who retaliated by entering the importer's domain. The wholesale merchants were not only selling in small quantities but were actively soliciting small accounts. Another factor was the declining relative importance of foreign manufactures. As the proportion of domestic goods sold increased

there was obviously less need for more than one stage in wholesaling.
Furthermore, as will be shown in a subsequent chapter, the latter
decades of the century saw a concerted effort on the part of
manufacturers, retailers, and consumers to eliminate some of the
middlemen and shorten the distribution channel.

Thus it was that before 1900 the movement toward a clear
distinction between the functions performed by importers, wholesale
merchants, and retailers had been largely completed. The so-called
traditional channel, manufacturer-wholesale merchant-retailer-
consumer, had been established and the wholesale merchant had assumed
those functions with which he is commonly associated today. These
will be discussed below in more detail.

Specialization by merchandise lines. As the possibilities for
specialization by products grew the wholesale merchants were quick to
take advantage of them. The following is a list of items in which
some wholesale merchants, selling at wholesale only, were
specializing by 1900. It provides an interesting comparison with the
similar data for 1860 presented in Chapter II page 31. These
should perhaps be regarded as more suggestive than all-inclusive:4

Books	Cheese
Boots and shoes	Children's clothing
Bottles and bottler's	China and glassware
supplies	Cigars
Butter and cheese	Clocks
Caps	Clothing
Carpets	Coal
Cement	Coffee and spices

(continued on next page)

Chairs	Confections
Charcoal	Jewelry, watches and plate
Crockery and glassware	Ladies underwear
Delicacies	Leather
Drugs	Linens
Drug sundries	Lumber
Dry goods	Men's furnishings
Fancy goods	Millinery goods
Fish	Notions
Floral	Overalls
Fruit	Pants
Glass	Paper
Groceries	Photographic supplies
Hats, caps, and furs	Plumber's supplies
Hardware	Rubber goods
Heavy hardware	Woolens
Hosiery	Wines and liquor
Iron and Steel	

The degree of specialization is determined by the size of the market. During the period 1860 to 1900 the markets were developing rapidly and it was this factor which was largely responsible for the acceleration of the tendency among wholesale merchants toward specialization by merchandise lines.

A more obvious factor, perhaps, in making possible this specialization by wholesale merchants was a similar trend among retailers. Since general stores had formerly been the typical retail outlet in the United States it had been necessary for the wholesale merchant to carry a relatively wide line in order to satisfy his customers' needs.[5] This situation in retailing was also, of course, a manifestation of the expansion of the markets. As the character of the markets changed and demand increased, the retail specialty store evolved. This phenomenon elicited the same development among wholesale merchants. It provided a possibility for product

specialization at the wholesale level and the merchants took
advantage of this.

The effects of these changes were to broaden and enlarge the
base of the structure of wholesale trade. Those engaged in
specialized operations became skilled in their work and as a result
efficiency was greater than it otherwise could have been.

Selling and Sales Promotion

Aggressive selling and sales promotion by wholesale merchants
was practically unknown before the Civil War. It is true, as shown
earlier, that traveling salesmen had been used but this was the
exception rather than the rule. Illustrated catalogs, special deals,
private brands, and similar promotional devices were all innovations
of the latter part of the nineteenth century. Advertising by
wholesale merchants, other than simple announcements of place of
business and type of goods handled, was extremely rare. The changing
nature of the markets and increasing severity of competition,
however, altered this situation considerably. Established trends
were strengthened and new ones started in selling and sales promotion
activity.

The development of traveling salesmen. By the close of the
Civil War the use of traveling salesmen was an established practice
with many of the leading firms of wholesale merchants. For example,
the Simmons Hardware Company was one of the first firms to send

salesmen on the road to sell goods. It began using salesmen about
1865. E.C. Simmons has said that:

> Previous to that we sent out men to collect
> for the goods sold previously and incidentally
> and occasionally they sold a few goods, but
> their main business was to collect and they were
> called collectors--not salesmen--although they
> sometimes took an order for goods, or rather had
> an order thrust upon them.[6]

The use of traveling salesmen spread rapidly. As indicated in
a preceding chapter there were only about 1,000 such representatives
in the United States in 1860.[7] By 1900 their number had reached over
92,000. The growth by decades was as follows:[8]

```
1860  ........................ 1,000
1870  ........................ 7,262
1880  ....................... 28,158
1890  ....................... 58,691
1900  ....................... 92,919
```

Of course, all of these salesmen were not employed by wholesale
merchants; some represented other types of wholesale middlemen as
well as manufacturers. Nevertheless, a large share were
representatives of merchant wholesalers and practically all were
selling at wholesale. Therefore the data are applicable in
illustrating the point.

By 1875 salesmen were calling on the trade everywhere and old
methods of doing business were being abandoned. It was not necessary
for the country merchant to make as frequent buying trips to the
central markets as he had in the past.

> The selling of goods, merchandise of every
> kind, and the means of having all branches of
> business, manufactures and industry represented
> through 'Traveling Salesmen' or 'Traveling
> Agents,' or, to use the word more generally
> given, 'Drummers,' or as termed in Great
> Britain, 'Commercial Travellers,'---has become
> in this country an almost universal and
> established system and rule, with every
> indication that it will even increase in its
> extent and variety rather than diminish.[9]

Not only were these salesmen numerous and widespread
geographically but they were important in virtually all lines of
trade by this time:

> By trunks, carpet-bags, valises, fully
> representing stocks of Dry Goods, Clothing,
> Furnishing Goods, Hats and Caps, Woolens, Fancy
> Goods, Small Wares, Groceries, Drugs, Medicines,
> Jewelry, Crockery and Glass-ware, Hardware,
> Boots and Shoes, and in fact every department of
> business which can be named, stocks on hand or
> to arrive are offered to the trade. Added to
> this the Furniture, Dealer, Carriage Builder,
> makers of machinery of every conceivable kind,
> by the aid of the Photographer, by Drawings or
> by the newly discovered Heliotype process may
> present designs from which to take orders,- all
> this understandingly, and if honorably
> conducted, to the mutual advantage of both buyer
> and seller.[10]

It was obviously recognized by many of the leading businessmen
during this period that traveling salesmen provided a good selling
tool. The salesmen were generally credited with bringing buyer and
seller closer together, reducing losses through bad debts, and making
collections more promptly. These are, of course, serious problems
for the present-day wholesalers but they were probably more serious
before 1900 because of the inadequacies in the transportation and

communication facilities of that time. It was felt that trade was extended and the prosperity of the various commercial centers enhanced through the efforts of these salesmen. Furthermore, some held that the efforts of the traveling salesmen tended to preserve and increase competition. Those who were concerned about the movement away from competition considered this effect advantageous for the economy as a whole.

It is clear then that the trend during this time was definitely toward the increased use of traveling salesmen as a means of reaching the markets. The reasons behind this trend can be divided logically and conveniently into two main groups. It was due to basic considerations of economic growth and to the nature of the competitive climate in which business operated that this refinement of the selling function took place so rapidly.

There was a considerable opposition in some lines of trade to the use of salesmen and this will be discussed below in some detail. Even those who opposed their use, however, recognized that drummers, as they were most commonly known, provided a quick and economical means of introducing new products to the markets. Since this was a period of rapid industrial development when new products were being marketed in increasing numbers, when the volume of manufactures was being doubled and redoubled, in short, a period of unprecedented economic growth, the environment was ideally suited to furthering the use of outside salesmen.

Improvements in transportation and communication facilities
went hand in hand with the above developments and provided a further
stimulus to the use of salesmen.

> The wonderful changes and progress which
> have been made during the present century, in
> the matter of public travel, may be of special
> interest to the young men of today to consider
> for upon these great changes, to a very great
> degree, is the present system of selling goods
> by 'Travelling Salesmen' attributable.[11]

In the first report on internal trade, 1876, it was pointed out
that commercial travelers were a relatively new "agency of commerce"
but had even by then become an established means of doing business.
It was further stated that "this new agency of commerce is now seen
to be a natural outgrowth of the facilities afforded by railroads and
telegraphs."[12]

It is more probable that the commercial travelers were a
"natural outgrowth" of the stage of economic development which was
being reached in the United States during this period. It is also
true, of course, that advances in transportation and communications
were a part of this development without which traveling salesmen
would not have been so widely used.[13] The rigors, expense, and time
involved in travel would have been prohibitive without these
facilitating agencies. Nevertheless, most of the contemporary
literature, as in the preceding examples, misplaces the emphasis in
discussing the reasons for the rapid rise of traveling salesmen. It

should lie also on the competitive situation as well as on the factors already cited.

Competition was both a cause and an effect in the development of these salesmen. The first travelers were employed by firms located in the eastern centers largely to meet the competition from the new centers being established in the interior. The latter met this competition in kind by employing their own drummers. Likewise competition within the individual wholesale market centers was intense and travelers were employed as a weapon in the battle among these firms. The "system of commercial travelers" was spawned by the economic and competitive situation and in turn served to heighten competition and to promote the economic growth of the country.

Although the influence and importance of the use of traveling salesmen in shaping the economy apparently was not generally recognized until later one authority had this to say in 1876:

> Every sale made by the commercial traveler tends to promote the prosperity of the city in which his business house is located, and to extend the commercial influence of that city. This creates competition with other commercial cities, and forces transportation lines to provide the requisite facilities to meet the new demands of trade. At the present time there are very few manufacturing or commercial houses in this country which do not employ one or more commercial travelers, and it is an indisputable fact that the energy, tact and persistency of these men have much to do in determining the direction of the commercial movements of the day.[14]

Such was the situation with regard to the rise of commercial
travelers and the factors responsible for that development. All was
not peace and quiet, however, for there were those who were violently
opposed to the new method and many did not hesitate to voice and
practice their objections. It is perfectly understandable, yet
interesting to note, that many of the critics were members of the
trades in which staple lines dominated, groceries for instance.

One of the most often repeated criticisms of salesmen as a
selling tool was the high cost. It was stated in 1880 that, "The
expenses of a first-class man to a wholesale house will average as
follows, when heavy baggage is not carried:[15]

```
Hotel bill ................... $2.00
Railroad fare  ..............   1.50
Bus and porterage  ..........    .75
Postage and telegrams ........   .25
Salary ......................   5.00
        Per diem ............. $9.50
```

Assuming the data to be accurate the total figure, viewed in
its proper perspective, is seen to be large. If salesmen's expenses
were to be held at three percent this would require a daily volume
per salesman of $317, if at five percent $190. With daily expenses
of $9.50, and assuming, for example, a gross margin of ten percent,
the sales would have to be $95 per day before any contribution to
other expenses and profits could have been made. These volumes were
apparently not unattainable for salesmen were widely used by this
time. Nevertheless, it was commonly said that even, "with the
strictest economy and prudence traveling expenses must and will be

large. These are closely scrutinized by all business concerns and
the almost universal exclamation is that selling goods away from home
is a very expensive way of doing business."[16]

A second commonly expressed criticism of traveling salesmen was
that they were ignorant of their lines and were not selected for their
real qualifications as salesmen but simply for their pertinacity in
soliciting orders. There was a good deal of truth in this objection
up until the time of John Henry Patterson and the beginning of his
work in "scientific" sales management in 1884. Before that time
salesmen were simply order takers who obtained business largely by a
process of hearty-back-slapping and story telling.

The selection of salesmen seems to have been primarily a process
of picking what the employer considered the "natural-born" salesman
from among his office or warehouse employees or from the ranks of his
competitors' sales staff. The biographies and autobiographies of many
of the successful merchants of subsequent decades show that they
became salesmen in the 1860's and 70's fresh from the wholesalers'
counting or stock rooms.

Formal training for wholesale salesmen was practically unthought
of during this period before Patterson's work. The sales manager
chose his salesmen, handed them a catalog and a sample case
admonishing them, perhaps, that their predecessor had been fired for
padding his expense account and they were ready to begin calling on
the trade.

The failure to recognize earlier the need for good selection, training, and supervision techniques was probably due to the relative ease with which the selling task could be accomplished. It is true, as indicated above, that competition was becoming more and more severe. Yet the jobbers' attention, for a long time after the Civil War, was focused more on the problem of securing goods with which to fill orders than securing the orders in the first place. As late as 1880 a prominent grocery wholesaler gave as one of his reasons for avoiding the use of traveling salesmen that:

> With a large force of salesmen constantly
> on the road in our line of business there is a
> constant tendency to oversell lines of goods in
> staple products where there is no exact
> standard, and in such cases the house has to use
> its best judgement in matching goods, which in
> all cases is not done satisfactorily.[17]

The following statement made in 1880 is interesting, as a commentary upon the operations of wholesale salesmen. It also shows that there had been some positive progress made in sales supervision before that time. John Henry Patterson is generally credited with being the first to establish exclusive or guaranteed sales territories. This may be true for commission men. The wholesalers, however, had followed this practice for sometime before, at least with their salaried salesmen:

> In order to cover well the territory
> tributary to a city a wholesale firm divides it
> up, and a specified route is given to each
> salesman which is known as his territory; this
> he speedily commences to work, and as he goes
> over and over it, he learns the character and

> peculiarities of the buyers; he informs
> himself of their financial status and method of
> conducting business, and soon becomes thoroughly
> conversant with his entire territory. He makes
> it a point to reach his customers just about the
> time they are needing goods and confidently
> calculates upon an order. He has always
> something new to present, or some attractive
> drive to offer, and will make a sale even though
> another man may have been just ahead in his same
> line. A warm business friendship soon springs
> up between buyer and seller, and it is as
> pleasant to the former to give an order as it is
> to the latter to receive it. A commercial
> traveler thus firmly established in confidence
> and esteem of his customers, holds well his
> trade in hand, and every year becomes more
> valuable to his principals.[18]

In 1895 the National Wholesale Druggists Association surveyed its members.[19] The purpose of the study was to discover the attitudes and practices of wholesale druggists concerning the use of traveling salesmen. Technically the study leaves a good bit to be desired yet much was uncovered that is of interest here.

The respondents, all of whom were wholesale druggists and members of the Association, though there undoubtedly was considerable diversity in scope and size of their operations, were asked to comment on the following points:

> 1. What are your views as to the
> limitation of a traveler's authority in the way
> of making allowances in the adjustment of
> complaints for overcharges, shortages, etc?
>
> 2. From your best experience in recent
> years, what do you expect from your best
> salesmen in gross sales per annum and what in
> gross profits? What from your least capable man
> in gross sales and profits? And what from the
> salesmen whose position strikes an average about
> halfway between the above?

3. What do you deem the proper limits of the expense account (including salary) of the three salesmen referred to above?

4. Do you consider the least capable man profitable to you?

5. Do you employ by salary and expense allowance or on a commission basis?

In regard to the first question, the making of adjustments and allowances by salesmen, eighty percent of the respondents were definitely opposed preferring to handle these matters from the home office. The other twenty percent favored giving the salesmen authority to handle such problems because of his closer contact with the retail customers.

The answers to the second question were less complete than the others because of the reticence of respondents to divulge what they considered confidential information. The data provided by those who answered (the number is not given) show the average sales per salesman ranged from $20,000 to $100,000. Forty thousand to $75,000 annual volume per salesman included the majority of the men reported upon. The gross profit reported on these sales averaged fifteen percent, the range being from 15 to 18 percent.

Contracts with salesmen were not commonly used, only one wholesale house stating that it had such contracts in force. Five-sixths of those answering stated that their compensation plans were based entirely on straight salary and expenses although it appeared that a number of these actually favored a commission basis for paying salesmen. The wholesaler used the straight salary while, in some cases, actually preferring a commission plan, undoubtedly because the former aided in controlling the salesmen more closely. The problem of control of the salesforce was, and is today, a serious one. In only one-sixth of the cases did these wholesalers report that they employed salesmen on a straight commission basis.

Thus the art of selling progressed and developed and the wholesale merchants continued to expand their forces of traveling salesmen. Meanwhile many divergent views were still being aired regarding the advantages and disadvantages of doing a wholesale business through traveling men. The whole thing was well summarized by a successful businessman and ex-traveling salesman of the period as follows:

> There seems to be a decided difference of opinion among businessmen as to the need of traveling salesmen. One merchant looks upon them as a help, another puts them under the head of a curse. One retailer thinks he buys cheaper because of them, but another is satisfied that traveling salesmen add an extra price to his bills. Some of the largest wholesale houses dispense with them entirely, while others systematize their trade so that it seems to be wholly dependent upon their traveling men. But whether this class of employees benefit trade or not, we may accept them as a necessary evil, and depend upon their remaining always with us.
>
> Just so long as some houses send out traveling men most houses must employ them. The firm that would dare to dispense with drummers today must be exceedingly sure of their customers, and must expect to be lavish with printed matter.....the great volume of trade is

> done through traveling men, and this way of
> doing business has its advantages if it has also
> its disadvantages.[20]

Catalogs and printed price lists as selling tools of the
wholesaler. Many of the severest critics of the use of traveling
salesmen by wholesale merchants suggested, as the best alternative,
the use of catalogs and printed price lists for soliciting business
which could not be handled by the house salesmen employed in every
firm. Most of the larger and more progressive wholesalers made use
of both methods of sale. They employed traveling salesmen furnishing
them with catalogs and price lists. They also mailed printed lists
and circulars to the trade at intervals to stimulate the mail order
business.

The Simmons Hardware Company, for example, had seventy-six
traveling salesmen on its payrolls in the early eighties.[21] In
addition, it regularly issued to retailers complete catalogs of its
lines and, of course, each of the salesmen carried one.[22] Simmons
states that the pioneer in developing wholesale catalogs was Markley,
Alling and Co. of Chicago which issued its first book in 1878 or
1879. His firm claims to have been the first to issue an illustrated
hardware catalog. It was printed in 1880 after eighteen months
preparation at a cost of $30,000. That this became a sizable catalog
is indicated by Saunders Norvell writing of his experience as a
Simmons traveling man between 1883 and 1892. He states, "I soon

found that I lost time and became tired out carrying my forty pound
hardware catalog around to the various stores in Denver."23

It would be correct to say that the era of illustrated catalogs
began about 1880. From that time catalogs have come to form an
indispensable tool in performing the sales task.

The catalog was an innovation made in response to the
increasing variety of goods appearing on the market during this time.
The lines handled by the larger wholesale firms were being
continually expanded and enlarged. It was not uncommon to find a
hardware wholesale merchant, for instance, with 10,000 or more items
in his line. Thus the catalog was born of necessity; it evolved from
the price lists which had been used previously and were subsequently
used as supplementary aids in selling.

In arguing for the abolition of the use of traveling salesmen
and extension of impersonal methods of solicitation of business by
wholesale merchants the Saint Louis Grocer of December 23, 1880
states:

> There is a grocery house in Saint Louis
> that have not had a traveling man upon the road
> for two years, except one who sells cigars and
> tobacco only, and they are at work from early in
> the morning until eleven o'clock at night,
> almost constantly, shipping and preparing goods
> for shipment.
>
> They do some business through local brokers
> and one or two commission salesmen, but mainly
> by issuing price-lists to the trade and
> advertising.

> We could mention quite a number of
> instances of 'old fogyism' of this kind, but
> will merely state that the 'era of quick travel
> and communication' assists these 'direct trade'
> merchants to reach 10,000 merchants once a week
> by mail, where ten traveling salesmen by fast
> work and making large points could not reach
> more than 100 merchants each per week, or 1,000
> merchant. The expense of these ten salesmen for
> the week would be very nearly $700, while that
> of the price-list would be about $150 per week.
> The ten salesmen would not sell more than
> one-quarter the merchants called upon, the price
> list will sell from five to ten percent of the
> merchants visited by it, or from 500 to 1,000
> orders weekly, against the 250 orders sold by
> salesmen.[24]

Thus catalogs and price lists came to be generally used before

1900. Some of the writers of this period were not above coloring the

data a bit if it served their purpose to do so. Such may be the case

with the preceding quotation; nevertheless, it does indicate the

extensive attention which was being given to this means of impersonal

solicitation of business.

Referring again to the foregoing quotation it is interesting to

note the implication that personal representation was more

satisfactory than catalogs and price lists in selling specialities

and breaking into new markets. The source was a grocery journal and

the firm mentioned was a grocery house. The goods in this trade were

largely staples and so the arguments presented do have some merit.

The trend toward the use of salesmen, at least in combination with

mail selling and advertising, was already well established and with

the broadening of markets, introduction of new products, larger

individual lines, and increasing competition, this movement was
stimulated until by 1900 the practice had become a part of the
operations of most of most wholesale merchants.

It is also true that there were other forces in operation by
1900 which were tending to reverse this trend and eventually led to
other innovations in wholesaling which de-emphasized the importance
of both traveling salesmen and mail selling. These factors will be
discussed in Chapter VI on the particular competitive problems met by
the wholesalers during the period under consideration.

The Early Development of Wholesalers' Brands

An innovation of this period was the placing of the
wholesaler's own brand on some of the goods which he handled. The
distributors', or private, brand is not uncommon today and the
advantages and disadvantages of such brands have been discussed
extensively. The pros and cons of the practice as it affects
wholesalers, manufacturers, and consumers are well known to students
of marketing. But what of the origin of the practice and the reasons
for its initial introduction and subsequent extension? The brand
policy to be considered here, of course, comes under the general head
of distributors' brands. Nevertheless, for purposes of clarity and
to distinguish from retailers' brands it is felt that the term
wholesalers' brands is best suited to the present discussion.

E.C. Simmons claims that his firm was the first to make use of
wholesalers' brands.[25] He states that the "era of special brands"

began in 1870 with the introduction in that year of the Simmons "Keen Kutter" axe. It may be true, perhaps, that Keen Kutter was the first wholesalers' brand name to be introduced in hardware but there were such brands in other lines which preceded Simmons.

Farrington, Brewster and Co., wholesale grocers in Chicago, for example, by 1870 were doing a "very large business, particularly in their own brands of smoking and chewing tobacco, known as Sans Souci."[26]

Another early distributor's brand was Ariosa coffee introduced in 1873 by Arbuckles and Company, wholesale grocers of Pittsburgh. This was the first successful national brand of package coffee. The original package coffee appears to have been Osborn's Prepared Java Coffee marketed in the early 1860's. Arbuckles began using premiums in 1895 to promote the sale of their Ariosa brand coffee.[27]

These are early examples of the use of distributors' brands. It was sometime, however, until the policy came into general usage. Wholesalers did not use their own brands to any considerable extent until around 1900 after which time the practice became more widespread. There were, of course, some exceptions to this, particularly among the larger wholesale firms.

The wholesale merchants, cited in the examples above, who early had their own brands were leaders in their respective fields, hardware and groceries. A similar example from the dry goods trade was the wholesale business of Marshall Field and Company which had been established as Field, Palmer and Leiter. This company not only handled its own brands before 1900 but controlled manufacturing facilities in which some of them were produced.[28]

The adoption of the distributors' brand policy by the wholesale merchants was an effort to get closer to the market, to build a reputation for the house and thus make for a more secure market position. In addition, margins on manufacturers' brand goods were small and manufacturers, especially in the last decade of the 19th century were attempting to bypass the wholesalers by selling direct to the retailers. All these things coupled with the difficulties arising out of the depression in the 1890's help to account for the acceleration at that time of the tendency toward the use of manufacturers' and distributors' brands.

Thus, even though wholesalers' brands were used relatively less before 1900 than later, there were factors developing before the turn of the century which stimulated a widespread use of such brands shortly thereafter. The fact that the wholesalers were, in general, doing well in the 1880's and 90's would seem to account in part for the lack of attention to development of their own brands. Furthermore, relatively few were large enough or had the resources necessary to acquire, finance, and promote their own brands.

Thus, this was a case of the introduction of new techniques of doing business before the business climate really necessitated their use. Once the factors favoring and making possible the use of distributors' brands became fully operative, and their advantages had been demonstrated, wholesale merchants soon put into practice the policy of selling goods under their own brands.

The Use of Advertising by the Wholesale Merchant

The economic situation in the sixties and early seventies was such that the wholesale merchants had little difficulty in securing business. Those who had goods could usually sell them at a reasonable profit. These conditions, however, did not persist. As has been pointed out, after the Civil War there was a gradual but constant shift from a sellers' to a buyers' market so that by about 1880 it had become necessary for sellers in most lines to solicit trade actively in order to carry on a profitable operation. Hence sales activities were constantly increased throughout the remainder of the century.[29]

Before 1880 advertising by wholesale merchants was definitely limited. Their efforts in advertising were confined largely to the insertion of small business cards in the various city directories. These advertisements as a rule contained only the name of the firm and the line in which it operated. Only very general, if any, mention was made of products, services or terms of sale being offered. As indicated there was also some use being made of direct mail in the form of price lists and, after 1870, catalogs were added to the wholesalers' arsenal of advertising weapons. In evaluating the advertising undertaken by wholesale merchants during this period it should be remembered that even up to 1900 advertising itself was still in its infancy and its efficiency and profitability had certainly not been clearly demonstrated.

Many wholesale firms attained large volumes of sales with little advertising, even in trade journals, or by means of direct mail solicitation of the trade. Printers' Ink in 1889 quotes a large wholesaler as giving as his reason for not advertising that:

> To be guilty of suggesting in an advertisement that they would like to sell more goods than they are now selling, or to sell to people who are not now customers, would be an admission of weakness, an acknowledgement, so to speak that the firm was not in a sound business condition. He seemed to think that it would be beneath their dignity as an old and conservative business firm to admit that they were in need of more customers or cared particularly to sell more goods.[30]

Whether this attitude was common or not it undoubtedly helps to account in part for the wholesale merchants' inattention to advertising before 1900.

In discussing the early advertising programs carried on by the Norvell-Shapleigh Hardware Company, which he helped form in 1901, Saunders Norvell states that he made extensive and profitable use of trade paper advertising.[31] He goes on to say, furthermore, that, "It has always surprised me that hardware jobbing houses did not do more advertising in our national and local papers."

This should not be taken to imply that there was no trade paper advertising done for such was not the case. The following data give the proportion of advertising carried in some of the leading trade papers in 1892. The figures represent the proportion of advertising to total space as found in one issue selected at random:[32]

Paper	Proportion of Advertising
Iron Age	75%
Northwestern Lumberman	59
Lumber Trade Journal	65
Shoe and Leather Review	86
Confectioner and Baker	75
Black Diamond	72 1/2
Street Railway Journal	69
Clothier and Furnisher	64
Carpet and Upholstery Review	69
Furniture Trade Review	74
American Artisan	63
Apparel Gazette	77
American Storekeeper	72 1/2
National Harness Review	60

In every case the proportion of advertising carried in these journals was over fifty percent of the total volume. The majority of the amount, however, appears to have been placed by manufacturers and not by wholesalers.[33]

Even in the case of manufacturers, although there were numerous instances of the use of advertising as a selling tool, few advertised in a consistent or systematic manner or over a very large area before the 1890's. In addition, practically nothing was done, either at the manufacturing or wholesale level, to integrate the advertising and selling programs. Merchandising the advertising was an untried technique.

One of the first instances of the now common practice of
merchandising the advertising was apparently in 1896 when one large
firm made news by adopting:

> A plan of sending its salesmen
> proofs of its advertisements as they were
> to appear in print. Two years later a
> leading dry goods house concluded that
> proofs of company advertising were just
> as important a part of the drummer's
> equipment as his samples. A portfolio of
> proofs was furnished each salesman and he
> was instructed on how to use it in
> instances when the merchant claimed there
> was no call for the merchandise. And it
> was found that this procedure helped
> sales immensely.[34]

By 1905 the techniques of merchandising the advertising had
become an integral part of practically every advertiser's
activities.

No discussion of changes and factors influencing changes in the
operations of wholesale merchants before 1900 would be complete
without a consideration of the impact of manufacturers' advertising
upon these operations. During the first two decades of the period in
question the wholesaler held the reins which guided the distributive
mechanism. The manufacturer sold to the wholesaler and beyond that
he knew practically nothing of his markets or the users of the goods
which he produced. This situation placed the wholesale merchant in a
dictatorial position from where he could, in many instances, tell the
manufacturer what and what not to do.

Thus the wholesale merchant was firmly entrenched and the manufacturer was operating, market-wise, at a disadvantage. The producers were not content with the relationships which existed between themselves and the middlemen. Some recognized that if they could identify themselves in the minds of the consumer with a quality product that they would be in a better position to deal with the trade. So the era of widely advertised manufacturers' brands began.

The movement began slowly at first but continued to gather speed. In the 1880's there were probably no more than a dozen manufacturing firms outside the patent medicine field who advertised on anything like a systematic continuing basis. There were, it is true, large numbers who advertised occasionally but their advertising was not a well-planned integrated part of the sales program. This picture changed rapidly during the nineties, however, and by 1900 there were a number of well-known manufacturers' brands for which a consumer preference had been established. Among these were Kodak, Heinz, Coca-Cola, Uneeda, Beeman's, Ingersoll, and Postum.[35]

This was a part of a general movement by manufacturers, referred to earlier, to get into closer contact with the ultimate consumer. The increasing quantity of output, the emergence of a buyers' market, inadequacies in the traditional distribution channel, and real and fancied abuses of the producer by the middlemen, all combined to bring about this effort by the manufacturer to get closer to the market. One of the obvious results was the extended use of

widely advertised manufacturers' brands which strengthened the
manufacturers' position in the market and in his relations with those
in the trade channel.

The purpose of this simplified analysis of the rise of
manufacturers' brands is to show how the wholesale merchants'
position in the channel was undermined and weakened by the
manufacturers' advertising and branding policies. The owner of the
branded or trade-marked good, once a consumer preference had been
established, was no longer at the mercy of the wholesalers. The
advertiser could, and did, in some instances before 1900, force his
product through the channel, so that if the wholesaler wanted to
supply his customers' needs he had no choice but to handle the brand.
In addition, the advertising of brands facilitated direct sale by the
manufacturer to the retailer or consumer.

The net effect was that the wholesale merchant instead of being
the dominant figure was placed on the defensive in his relations with
the manufacturer. The natural outcome was increased promotion by the
wholesale merchant of his own brand goods. This, obviously, was the
genesis of the so-called "Battle of the Brands" which became very
intense after about 1910. Other ramifications and effects of the
changing status of the wholesale merchant during the last two decades
of the nineteenth century will be discussed later in connection with
the analysis of the particular competitive problems which arose at
the time for the wholesale middleman.

There is little information available concerning the techniques used by the wholesale merchant before 1900 in budgeting, planning, and preparing his advertising program. As a matter of fact it is highly probable that a thorough study made in the nineties of the methods used at that time would have shown little or no systematized advertising, planning, and programming in use by the wholesaler.

It is probable, then, that during the period 1860-1900 the amount spent by the wholesale merchants for advertising was small. The bulk of their selling efforts were directed through the medium of traveling salesmen. The advertising program was not well organized, but it must be borne in mind that advertising as a sales tool was still in its infancy throughout the business world. The major portion of the wholesale merchants' early advertising was confined to signs, price bulletins, and circulars. Later these came to include house organs, catalogs, some direct mail announcements other than price lists, and advertisements in trade magazines. Up to 1900 these advertisements consisted largely of simple announcements of place of business, name of firm and the like with now and then a mention of major lines handled or service offered. The small amount of consumer advertising done by these wholesalers was to support their own brands but the major developments in this did not take place until after 1900.

The Wholesale Merchant's Credit Operations

One of the major functions performed by the wholesale merchant during the period under consideration was the extension of credit to the retailer. Including checks as credit instruments it was estimated that in 1897 over ninety percent of all sales were made on a credit basis.[36] This service by the wholesale merchant represented an important source of financial aid for the retailer. It also created major problems for the wholesale merchant. Because of the nature and importance of these credit operations it seems expeditious to subdivide the topic for more detailed consideration.

Obtaining credit information. Because of the lack of dependable credit information before 1900 the wholesale merchant was often forced to make his credit decision on the basis of very meager data. There were a number of common sources of information but they were all subject to much criticism.

One of the more important sources was credit reports by the wholesale merchants' salesmen. One businessman writing in 1890 said that, "A very large proportion of the credits throughout the country are made directly by agents, or based on their opinions, and in a large measure the prosperity of most houses is in their hand."[37]

It is not difficult to understand the reason salesmen were relied upon for much credit information when one recalls the evolution of the traveling man. As explained previously the earliest commercial travelers were employed as collection agents. Thus even

after the selling function began to occupy the majority of his
attention the salesman was still expected to, and did, devote a
portion of his time to collecting, making adjustments, and preparing
credit reports for his employers. As a matter of fact, this
expectation still persists today though to a somewhat lesser degree.

The salesman was often criticized for his shortcomings as a
credit reporter. It was said that if the traveling men did "less
business for glory, and more for profit, there would not be so much
need of lawyers among businessmen."[38]

The mention of lawyers obviously referred to their use in
collecting past due and delinquent accounts.

Probably the major reason for the lack of confidence in the
salesmen as credit men was that too much was expected of them. By
1900 the attitude of the firm toward its salesmen's credit reporting
had become more rational. One wholesale credit manager writing in
1907 states that:

> Salesmen afford a valuable source of
> information, if the credit men will take the
> trouble to educate them to the observation and
> collection of the kind of information he
> desires. It can hardly be expected that the
> good salesman will also be a good credit
> man--especially in the same transaction.[39]

A second major source of information for wholesale merchants
during this period was the commercial agencies. Skinner states that
the first source of credit data for the wholesale merchant was the
rate books of the commercial agencies. The next most common source

was the special reports of these agencies which were useful even
though admittedly they were not entirely current.[40]

By 1890 the mercantile agency system was a well-established and
generally accepted part of the business structure. In spite of a
determined opposition from some quarters of the business public the
agencies had demonstrated their ability to perform a useful service:

> But notwithstanding all the shortcomings of
> the system, and with all its glaring defects, it
> is, nevertheless, a permanent institution with
> the American business-public, and has come to
> stay..... Within the last few years the agency
> has been accorded a place in the business
> community of this country at least, and by
> reason of this recognition they have been able
> to assume a more independent attitude.[41]

As evidence that these agencies did not receive universal
acclamation it is interesting to note some of the writings of the
critics. Exemplary of these were Meagher, The Commercial Agency
System Exposed, and Chinn, Mercantile Agencies Against Commerce.[42]
Among other things these authors characterized the agencies as
secret, treasonous, inquisitorial organizations whose investigations
and reports were made to suit their own pocketbooks. The agencies
were charged with furnishing information which was only a highly
diluted form of hearsay and with contributing to panics and other
major disasters.

Although the system was undoubtedly subject to abuse and some
of the charges may have been based on fact, it is undeniable that the
agencies performed a real and necessary service for the wholesalers

and other businessmen. One needs only to observe the growth of the
credit reporting companies and their subscriber lists for
substantiation of this fact.

In 1860 much of the wholesale business of the country was done
on a personal basis:

> The retail buyer had no general credit; he
> established relations with one or two
> wholesalers who made themselves familiar with
> his character, his ability, and the conditions
> under which he made his sale. The fabric of the
> trade was built up upon this intimate knowledge
> of personality, which often resulted in the
> complete assumption of a buyer's indebtedness by
> a single wholesaler in each of the merchandise
> lines which he handled, dry goods, groceries,
> leather goods, hardware, etc.[43]

As the economy grew and with the widening of markets and
lengthening of channels of trade some provision for the interchange
of credit information became essential. The personal relationships
between the wholesale merchant and his customers became more
infrequent and less intimate so it was natural that resort should be
had to the mercantile agencies for information formerly gathered
first-hand but now unavailable by that means.

A source of credit information similar to the mercantile
agencies was those organizations formed within the various
associations of wholesalers. An instance of this cooperation was in
the drug trade. It is described in the 1895 report of the Credit and
Collections Committee of the National Wholesale Druggists
Association. The detailed picture is interesting:

Many of the Western exchanges have
organized what is known as a "credit clearing
house." These credit clearing house rules
consist of regulations which have been carefully
considered, and which have been in practical
operation in some of the exchanges for several
years. By these rules a systematic interchange
of experience is made possible between the
various credit departments of the members of the
exchanges. This is done without in any way
giving valuable information to a competitor as
to the details of the jobber's business, and at
the same time is equitable and mutually
beneficial. The results enable the members
to compile reports which will show the total
trade liabilities and dealings of their
customers, and to render it more impossible for
unsafe credits to multiply, or for a dishonest
dealer to overbuy and get his goods, or for a
dealer who disregards his obligations with one
house to purchase from another; in other words,
to furnish a "clearing house" for the records
and experiences of credit men which will supply
them with the missing link in their present
chain of information; thus weeding out in time
the undesirable dealers, who are not only a
source of annoyance and direct loss to the
wholesalers, but who furnish such undue
competition for the honest, fair-dealing
merchant, from whom the wholesalers must
necessarily obtain their profit.[44]

Along with the above sources of credit information the

wholesale merchant also used local attorneys and banks to help him

overcome the perennial problem of determining to whom credit should

be extended. Considerable progress was made before 1900 in working

toward a solution to this problem. It was estimated in 1896 that bad

debt losses though varying by lines of trade ranged, in general, from

four to eight-tenths of one percent of credit sales.[45] Taken alone

this is admittedly not a conclusive index of credit department efficiency. Nevertheless, considering the difficulties under which the credit function was carried on and the fact that during a large part of the period 1860-1900 credit was relatively easily available the low bad debt loss is an indication, at least, of efficient credit department operations. It is also apparently true that the major advances since 1900 in the process of securing credit information have been refinements in techniques already in use rather than the addition of new methods.

Credit terms. Although the credit period in 1860 ranged from four to six and even up to twelve months in length, there was at that time a discernible trend toward a shortening of the time allowed for payment. This general tendency continued throughout the period up to 1900.

Wholesale merchants were universally aware of the evils inherent in the overlong credit periods and were anxious to sell on shorter terms. The experience and action of the wholesale druggists on this are illustrative of those of many of the other trades.

The Western Wholesale Drug Association, forerunner of the National Wholesale Druggists Association, was formed in 1876. At this time terms were not uniform and although they had been shortened considerably "a year's time was not infrequent in the pioneering country west of the Mississippi where some of the mountain dealers were obliged to wait from three to six months for deliveries...."[46]

At its first meeting the Association after considerable debate passed the resolution that, "all credit be shortened as soon and as much as practicable; and that the goods being sold on the least profit be, as a rule, sold on the shortest time."[47] The debate concerning the resolution showed that many members favored 30 days with one percent for cash as ideal terms but these were not adopted by the Association as ideal terms until 1887.

By 1900 the terms in use in the wholesale drug trade were 1 1/2 percent for cash in ten days, net sixty days. The credits and collections committee of the Association devoted a major portion of its report in 1900 to expounding the desirability of shortening these terms further to thirty days and one percent for cash.[48]

This represents a considerable reduction in the length of the credit period in the drug trade, from as long as one year in 1860 to sixty days in 1900. Other lines of trade were experiencing similar reductions. There were a number of factors which contributed to this shortening of the time for which wholesale merchants were willing to extend credit.

A major cause was the uncertainty of conditions during and following the Civil War, and the highly fluctuating value of the monetary unit up until the resumption of specie payments in 1879. The danger that he would be paid in currency that was worth less than it had been at the time of sale of the goods led the wholesale merchant to shorten his terms and to offer a discount for prompt payment. It is inevitable that uncertainty and an unstable currency situation should have this result. The gravity of the general situation led the National Wholesale Druggists Association to make the following declaration in 1878:

> Your committee would further call attention to the burdensome and unjust expense to which the trade have been subjected by the custom of remitting in payment of bills, checks, on country banks, which can only be used at a discount, and to the custom of remitting by express without prepayment of charges, and to the further custom that has obtained of drawing drafts without exchange. We, therefore, recommend that the trade adopt as their rule and custom:
>
> First:--To receive checks on distant banks at their bankable value.
>
> Second:--That all moneys sent per express must be prepaid, or at the expense of the sender.
>
> Third:--That all drafts drawn in payment of bills or accounts should be with the words with current rate of exchange.[49]

The continued use of the shorter terms which grew out of the unsettled economic and monetary conditions of the Civil War was facilitated by the development of railroad transportation and rapid means of communication. The railroad and telephone and telegraph made it possible to complete a transaction much more rapidly than had been feasible previously, thus removing the physical barriers to shorter terms. The trend away from the agricultural to the industrial type of economy was another important facilitating factor.

In agricultural areas credit was offered for longer periods and long terms were still common after 1900 in the sale of agricultural machinery. The resumption of specie payments in 1879 and the shift to a buyers' market at about the same time appear to have slowed the trend somewhat but did not stop it.

Financial assistance to retailers. One of the functions commonly performed by wholesale merchants during this period was the giving of financial assistance to retailers. This was accomplished primarily by means of the extension of credit as discussed above.

It was not uncommon to find the wholesale merchant providing capital for a retailer just getting started in business. So-called "opening stocks" were, in many cases, sold on long terms. Probably this credit made it possible for many stores to be established which could not otherwise have ever been opened.

One of the leading dry goods wholesalers before 1900 was the Claflin Company of New York. This company was particularly active in extending credit and promoting credit sales. Mr. Edward D. Page, himself a leading dry goods merchant, in analyzing the Claflin operations states that a number of Claflin's customers were originally supported by his credit and financial assistance.[50] Similar policies were pursued by Field, Leiter and Company, the forerunner of Marshall Field and Company, and by most of the other leading firms.[51]

The only conclusive way to quantify the extent of the financial
assistance rendered the retailer would be to analyze data on the
percent of the wholesalers' capital tied up in accounts receivable.
Unfortunately, there are no such data available for the period under
consideration. The earliest such information that was found pertains
to 1927 in the wholesale dry goods trade:[52]

| | Percent of Assets |
Invested Capital	Represented by Accounts Receivable
Less than $250,000	37.1
$250,000 to $500,000	41.8
$500,000 to $1,000,000	41.7
$1,000,000 and over	34.5

These figures show a considerable proportion of the wholesale
merchants' capital in the hands of the retailers in the form of
credits on merchandise. In the grocery trade the percentage exceeded
fifty and in the coal business considerably more than that. It is a
reasonable assumption, then, that before 1900 in most trades probably
more than half the wholesalers' capital was invested, via
receivables, in the retailers' business. This conclusion is borne
out by the already established facts that terms then were much longer
than after 1900 and that a larger percentage of the wholesale
business was conducted on a credit basis.

It is apparent that the wholesaler offered an important service
in making financial aid available to retailers during a period of
rapid growth and development. This activity might more properly fall
under the heading of banking. However, many retailers could not have

qualified for credit from other sources so the wholesale merchant supplied it. In so doing he was performing a vital function.

Physical Facilities and Organization

Facilities. The physical plant in which the wholesaler conducted his operations between 1860 and 1900 was inefficient judged by later standards. Looked at in the light of contemporary economic conditions and considerations, however, sound reasons become apparent for the developments which took place.

Early in the development of wholesaling in the United States the wholesale merchants' warehouses were located along waterfronts for easy access to the principal means of transportation. These early buildings were mostly one-story in height but by 1860 this had changed considerably. Between 1860 and 1900 the tendency was to multi-story structures. This trend continued up until recently when it was again reversed, in certain areas and lines, in favor of one story units located on outlying sites.

The reason for the multi-story building was largely economic. As the market centers expanded the cost of ground rose and the cost for large building sites become prohibitive. The obvious solution was taller buildings, generally with low ceiling and a number of floors. The use of the elevator, which had been introduced in the 1850's, undoubtedly did much to keep down the cost of operations in these buildings.[53] Goods were not stacked high and the low ceilings increased the number of square feet of floor space which could be placed in a building of a given size.

As the railroad net developed wholesale merchants tended to move from the waterfronts to sites near the railroad yards. Instead of building new and more efficient buildings, however, they took over buildings which had been erected for manufacturing or other purposes.

A recent study of warehousing in the wholesale drug field bears out the above statement:

> The predominance of multi-story building in the wholesale drug trade seems to be due to the following factors:
>
> 1. A majority of firms were established long ago when most wholesaling was centered in the market places so as to be convenient to communication and transportation centers. In such locations competition for space was sharp, resulting in high land values, consequently, buildings "went up" in order to get the desired floor space on a limited ground area.
>
> 2. Many wholesalers moved into buildings which were erected for manufacturing or other non-wholesaling purposes.
>
> 3. Not until recently have drug wholesalers begun to realize the advantages of the one-floor operation over the multi-floor operation.[54]

In 1887 Marshall Field erected new quarters for his wholesale firm in Chicago covering the entire block between Adams, Franklin, Quincy and Wells streets; the building contained eight floors and a basement.55 The following is an interesting description of

facilities in the wholesale grocery trade in 1895:

> Beginning with the building itself, the
> great grocery firms of New York are similar in
> that they occupy their own homes, some of them
> covering the greater part of a city
> block--enormous ten-story buildings where from
> basement to top story is stored the most complex
> stock to be found outside of a department store;
> lighted by electric lights, reached by
> fast-running elevators....On the ground floor is
> located the shipping department, where from
> twenty to twenty-five great two-horse trucks and
> delivery wagons can be loaded at once with
> expedition and accuracy. Another floor is
> usually given over to the offices and
> countingrooms, handsomely finished off, where a
> force of clerks, the pay of whom alone would
> have swamped the old-time merchant, is kept busy
> recording the infinite detail of the firm's
> transactions.56

There are no well-written descriptions available of the systems

used in the early wholesale warehouses. Saunders Norvell's

description of the methods in use in the early 1880's when he went to

work for Simmons Hardware Company of St. Louis, however, provides an

insight into one important phase of operations, that of assembling

orders:

> After that I became order clerk and began
> to learn the business as I handled the
> salesmen's original orders. In those days the
> orders were handled by the stock clerks on the
> third floor in deals. In starting to work a
> deal the first thing we did was to copy all the
> goods of the other departments in small books
> provided for the purpose. These books were sent
> to the various departments and were returned
> with the goods in trucks. With this system the
> stock clerk on the third floor handled the goods
> of practically every department, got them

> together, laid them out on tables and when the
> bill was finished and every item was complete,
> he called for a "hear-back" to check up the
> bill. This gave us an opportunity to learn all
> the various departments of the business.[57]

Considering the available information then it is apparent that
the wholesale merchants' physical facilities and handling operations
were neither efficient nor economical in terms of presently accepted
standards. Yet to properly assess their efficiency we must evaluate
it in the light of the best methods then known and available.
Considered in this way the wholesale merchants' physical operations
seem to have been fairly efficient. However, it appears that less
progress was made, between 1860 and 1900, in coping with the problems
related to this function than with some of the others which the
wholesale merchant performed. The reason was that comparatively
little attention seems to have been devoted to finding means of
improving efficiency in the methods of receiving and shipping goods,
probably because the labor used in this operation was relatively
cheap. Perhaps if the wholesale merchant had regarded his warehouse
less as a storage bin and more as a place through which the goods
necessarily had to be moved as efficiently as possible more progress
would have been made.

As a matter of fact, the wholesale merchant was preoccupied
with other problems and was undoubtedly devoting his time to those
tasks which seemed most urgent and where profit possibilities
appeared greatest. These were functions such as buying, selling,

advertising, and credit and collections, in which increased
efficiency was achieved. This accounts in part, at least, for the
lack of attention to the performance of the storage functions.

Organization. Like the storage function the problem of
organization in the wholesale firm received less attention before
1900 than did other aspects of the business.

For one thing most wholesale firms started out as small
businesses in which the proprietor or partners performed most of the
work themselves. As the firm grew little attention was paid to
careful separation of tasks. Where division was made it was often
done on the basis of personalities in the business rather than along
logically consistent lines. As late as 1901, in describing the
organization of the buying in the newly-founded Norvell-Shapleigh
Hardware Company, Norvell complains that some of the officers
insisted upon performing a part of the buying function. It required
considerable time and several major mistakes before they were
convinced that the buying authority and responsibility should be
centered in the hands of a specialist.[58]

Furthermore, it remained for the founders of the scientific
management movement, beginning in the 1880's, to point out the
techniques and advantages of careful attention to management and
organizational structure. Even after that the wholesale merchant was
slow to alter the traditional practices. It was really not until
after 1900 under increasing competitive pressure that the wholesale

merchant began to give careful attention to problems of organization and management.

One notable movement before 1900 in this general area of organization, however, was the increasing number of incorporations by wholesale firms. An interesting discussion of this is provided by E. C. Simmons:

> The era of Hardware incorporation is a most interesting bit of history. Simmons Hardware Company was incorporated January 1, 1874, and was the first commercial or jobbing house in any branch of business in the United States to incorporate. How the fact was ridiculed and jeered at is well remembered by many who are still in the Hardware trade, and the records of the mercantile agencies show that the "experiment" was looked upon with grave suspicion as an effort to evade personal responsibility and liability--in fact it was openly discussed that this new move of "Simmons" was a wicked scheme, preparing for dishonest failure. It is not necessary to speak of what followed, for everybody knows that corporations became fashionable in the Hardware world, both wholesale and retail, and today are largely the rule rather than the exception. Perhaps some of your readers have often wondered why there were more incorporations in the Hardware line than in any other kind of business, which is the fact. The answer is very easy, because the corporation idea originated with the hardware merchant, as explained above. Hardware manufacturers were incorporated long ago, but Hardware merchants not until 1874.[59]

It is possible that Simmons' claims that his was the first wholesale firm to incorporate could be refuted. Nevertheless, this was an early instance of such incorporation and the comments provide an interesting insight into the attitudes of the time. After this incorporations by wholesale merchants became more common.

Changing Status of Shipping Merchants, Importers and Exporters

Decline of the shipping merchant. After the Civil War the shipping merchant declined in importance.[60] One observer states that by 1892 the old shipping merchants of New York had disappeared and "they left no successors."[61] He defined shipping merchants as ship owners who bought and sold merchandise, transported it in their own ships, and took the risks involved in these operations.

In its review of fifty years of commerce the report of the Boston Board of Trade in 1862 furnishes further evidence of the declining importance of shipping merchants. It indicates that the merchant, "who not only owned his ships, but the cargoes inward and outward," had occupied an important place in Boston commerce before 1860 but became less prominent thereafter. These merchants had been classified according to the country in whose goods they specialized; there had been among others, East India, West India, and Mediterranean merchants.[62]

Thus, although the shipping merchants apparently had occupied an important place in wholesaling before the Civil War it is clear that they decreased markedly in importance thereafter.

Reasons for the decline. There were a number of reasons for this change. In the first place shipping merchants were engaged primarily in foreign trade. Following the Civil War internal trade expanded rapidly and more and more attention was being centered on promoting its development. This tended to overshadow the importance of foreign trade and the institutions engaged in that trade.

Furthermore, other nations were providing serious competition for American shipping. In 1867 a writer gave the following reasons for the decline:

> The war left us with depreciated currency, high prices of materials and labor, and a burdensome system of taxation. These evils still continue, and in a modified form may be expected to continue for some time to come. They affect all branches of industry among us; but all except the shipping interest, have reserved strength upon which to fall back, while it alone has to meet the encounter in an utterly prostrate condition. Moreover, our ships have to compete in the maritime centres of the globe with ships built on a gold basis, at comparatively low cost of labor and materials, and under exemption from all taxes on construction, outfit, repairs and stores. Our wool growers, our manufacturers, our iron masters, with heavy protective duties find it difficult upon their own soil, under existing circumstances, to compete with the industry of other nations. Is it strange, then, that our shipowners find it altogether impossible, in the absence of friendly legislation, to compete with the foreign owner....?[63]

The United States merchant marine had been seriously reduced in size during the Civil War and foreign shipping was gradually taking over from American interests the carrying of American imports and exports. The shipping merchants had owned the ships in which their goods were carried. They had difficulty in competing with the foreign firms who specialized in transportation and could, for this reason and those mentioned in the preceding quotation, apparently perform this function more efficiently than could the merchant. Thus, it is probable that the shipping merchants found it increasingly desirable to reduce their investments in ships in order to have more capital available for their merchandising or other operations.

The increasing size of manufacturing and business firms in the United States also tended to make the position of the shipping merchant less tenable and contributed to his decline. As the firms grew larger they were in a position to deal directly with foreign suppliers and to sell in foreign markets without the services of the shipping merchants. The American firms who specialized in importing also provided serious competition for this aspect of the shipping merchants' operations.

It is probable, then, that even without the serious effects of the Civil War the shipping merchant would have declined in importance. Business firms were growing larger and becoming more capable of handling their own foreign transactions. The shipping merchant did not specialize by commodities and he performed both a transportation and merchandising operation. Firms specializing by commodities and/or functions could operate more effectively. Thus, commission, banking, importing, and transportation specialists appear to have furnished severe competition for these merchants. Improvements in communications with foreign countries also made it

easier for American firms to deal directly with those countries
further weakening the position of the shipping merchant.

Importers and Exporters

The tendency among importers to specialize by commodities was
apparent in 1860.[64] This trend continued after the Civil War but the
position of the importer was weakened by increasing participation of
other types of organizations in the importing business, by high
tariffs, and by increasing competition from domestic goods.

Among manufacturers there was an increasing tendency to import
goods themselves. During this period a number of firms advertised
themselves as importers and manufacturers of a particular line.
There were also those who advertised that they were importers and
wholesalers, or importers, wholesalers, and retail dealers.[65] This
would seem to indicate that some of the wholesale merchants handling
domestic goods were also doing some importing on their own account.[66]
It is also probable that some of these were importers who undertook
to sell to retailers. Copeland found in his study that by 1917 the
predominant importers of cotton products in New York were American
jobbers and retailers.[67]

As shown in Table IX the volume of exports increased after the
Civil War and usually exceeded the volume of imports. However, the
export merchants, the individuals or firms selling abroad on their
own account, apparently did not increase rapidly in number or size

TABLE IX

VALUE OF MERCHANDISE* IMPORTS AND EXPORTS, UNITED STATES, 1860-1900

	Imports	Exports	Excess of Exports	Excess of Exports
1860	$353,616,119	$333,576,057	$ 20,040,062	
1861	289,310,542	219,553,833	69,756,709	
1862	189,356,677	190,670,501		1,313,824
1863	243,335,815	203,964,447	39,371,368	
1864*	316,447,283	158,837,988	157,609,295	
1865	238,745,580	166,029,303	72,716,277	
1866	434,812,066	348,859,522	85,952,544	
1867	395,761,096	294,506,141	101,254,955	
1868	357,436,440	281,952,899	75,483,541	
1869	417,506,379	286,117,697	131,388,682	
1870	435,958,408	392,771,768	43,186,640	
1871	520,223,684	442,820,178	77,403,506	
1872	626,595,077	444,177,586	182,417,491	
1873	642,136,210	522,479,922	119,656,288	
1874	567,406,342	586,283,040		18,876,698
1875	533,005,436	513,442,711	19,562,725	
1876	460,741,190	540,384,671		79,643,481
1877	451,323,126	602,475,220		151,152,094
1878	437,051,532	694,865,766		257,814,234
1879	445,777,775	710,439,441		264,661,666
1880	667,954,746	835,638,658		167,683,912
1881	642,664,628	902,377,346		259,712,718
1882	724,639,574	750,542,257		25,902,683
1883	723,180,914	823,839,402		100,658,448
1884	667,697,693	740,513,609		72,815,916
1885	577,527,329	742,189,755		164,662,426
1886	635,436,136	679,524,830		44,088,694
1887	692,319,768	716,183,211		23,863,443
1888	723,957,114	695,954,507	28,002,607	
1889	745,131,652	742,401,375	2,730,277	
1890	789,310,409	857,828,684		68,518,275
1891	844,916,196	884,480,810		39,564,614
1892	827,402,462	1,030,278,148		202,875,686
1893	866,400,922	847,665,194	18,735,728	
1894	654,994,622	892,140,572		237,145,950
1895	731,969,965	807,538,165		75,568,200
1896	779,724,674	882,606,938		102,882,264
1897	764,730,412	1,050,993,556		286,263,144
1898	616,049,654	1,227,023,302		615,432,676
1899	697,148,489	1,227,023,302		529,874,813
1900	849,941,184	1,394,483,082		544,541,898

*Gold and Silver not separately stated prior to 1864.
Source: Treasury Department, Bureau of Statistics, The Foreign Commerce and Navigation of the United States (Washington: Government Printing Office, 1902), p. 49.

and even after 1900 there were "very few real export merchants in
this country."[68]

Some firms carried on an export commission business and
manufacturers had export departments which handled their foreign
sales. Some of these had branches in other countries; the Industrial
Commission reported in 1900 that:

> The most successful exporters of American
> products have found it desirable to establish
> permanent agencies in leading foreign markets,
> and to push the sale of their goods directly.
> Such permanent agencies are able to adapt
> themselves to local conditions, to watch for
> favorable opportunities, to advertise by
> suitable methods, and to give more earnest
> attention to the extension of trade than can be
> expected from mere commission agents or from
> traveling salesmen.[69]

It is probable that the reason the export merchant did not
experience a greater development between 1860 and 1900 was two-fold.
In the earlier part of the period domestic markets easily absorbed
the product of American industry and so American merchants preferred
to sell at home rather than enter the foreign market in which selling
was more difficult. A Congressional investigating committee
concluded in 1885 that:

> The true reason for the lack of commerce in
> the countries to which the attention of the
> commission has been directed is that the
> commercial enterprise of the American people has
> found the requirements of our own vast and
> increasing population so great as to absorb,
> until recently, all they were able to produce;
> and our merchants, from the promptings of
> self-interest, have left the more complex field
> of foreign commerce to be cultivated by the

> merchants of countries whose internal demands
> have been less than those of the United
> States.[70]

By this time, however, manufacturers were large enough, in many cases, to conduct their own export operations so that there was then little need for numerous large firms of export merchants.

Summary

During the period 1860 to 1900 the wholesale merchant was one of the more important intermediaries in the internal trade of the United States. Although by 1900 some wholesale merchants still operated as semi-jobbers, the larger and more important ones were selling at wholesale only. The trend toward specialization by merchandise lines continued throughout this time till by 1900 it was not uncommon to find firms specializing not only by general lines but concentrating on particular classes of goods within each trade. This was made possible by the increasing variety and quantity of goods being manufactured, by increases in the size of the markets for these products, and by specialization among the retailers to whom the wholesale merchant sold.

The wholesale merchant devoted considerable time and attention to developing new techniques of selling and sales promotion during this time. Traveling salesmen, or drummers, came into common use and were instrumental in building large volumes for the business firms which they represented. The method of sale was changed considerably, if not entirely. By about 1880 salesmen were traveling in every corner of the country, whereas, twenty years before it was the

practice for country merchants to come to the central market to do
their buying. Selling aids such as printed price lists, catalogs,
direct mail circulars, and so on, were widely used during these
latter decades. Less use was made of other types of advertising
until after 1900 when wholesalers' brands became more common.

The increased emphasis on the selling function and use of more
aggressive methods of sale were due to the increasing competitive
pressure under which the wholesale merchant operated. The sellers'
market of the Civil War gradually gave way to a buyers' market.
Transportation and communication facilities were continually
expanding and bringing the wholesale merchants in the various centers
into closer competition.

In the forty years following 1860, then, the wholesale merchant
became important as a vital link in the common trade channel,
manufacturer-wholesale merchant-retailer-consumer. Those four
decades were not without their serious problems for the wholesale
merchant; yet they were generally prosperous years.

The shipping merchant declined in importance in the face of
competition from specialists in the functions which he had performed.
He did not specialize but carried on a general operation. The
position of the importer was weakened by the increasing participation
of other types of organizations in the importing business, by high
tariffs, and by increasing competition from domestic goods. For the

reasons mentioned the export merchant experienced only a limited
development.

In the next chapter attention will be given to the changing
status of another type of wholesale intermediary, the agent
middleman. In Chapter VI attention will be devoted to the particular
competitive problems encountered by both merchant and agent
wholesalers and the methods used in meeting them.

FOOTNOTES - CHAPTER IV

[1]See Chapter I, p. 5.

[2]Fred M. Jones, "Middlemen in the Domestic Trade of the United States," Illinois Studies in the Social Sciences, Vol. 21:3, May, 1937, p. 13.

[3]The Banker's Magazine, Vol. X (New Series), January, 1861, p. 569.

[4]From an examination of various business directories including: Boston Register and Business Directory, 1899-1900; Gopsill's Philadelphia City Directory, 1899; Chicago City Directory, 1904; The Trow Business Directory of Greater New York, 1906; Baltimore Directory, 1899; Boston Directory, 1899.

[5]Jones, op. cit., p. 45. See also J.S. Currey, Manufacturing and Wholesale Industries of Chicago (Chicago: Thomas B. Poole, Co., 1918), Vol. I, p. 415.

[6]E.C. Simmons, "A Half Century of Hardware," Iron Age, January 4, 1906, p. 146.

[7]See page 36.

[8]The figure for 1860 is an estimate from E.P. Briggs, Fifty Years on the Road; the rest of the data are from the Bureau of the Census, decennial censuses of population, which first began reporting "Commercial Travelers" in its tables of occupations in 1870.

[9]William H. Baldwin, Travelling Salesmen (Boston, 1874), p. 1.

[10]Loc. cit.

[11]Ibid., p. 6.

[12]Annual report of the Chief of the Bureau of Statistics, Part II, Internal Commerce and Transportation, 1876 (Washington, 1877), p. 66.

[13]Melvin T. Copeland, "Managerial Factor in Marketing," in Facts and Factors in Economic History (Cambridge: Harvard University Press, 1932), p. 601.

[14]Annual Report of the Chief of the Bureau of Statistics, op. cit., p. 66.

[15]J. Nimmo, Jr., Report on the Internal Commerce of the United States, 1880 (Washington, 1881), Appendix No. 24, p. 208, quoting the St. Louis Grocer, December 23, 1880.

[16]Baldwin, op. cit., p. 14.

[17]"Statement prepared by Mr. F.B. Thurber of the wholesale grocery house of H.K. and F.D. Thurber and Co., of New York in Regard to the Policy of Conducting Trade Through the Agency of Commercial Travelers," in J. Nimmo, Jr., op. cit., p. 205.

[18]Ibid., p. 208.

[19]National Wholesale Druggists Association, Proceedings of the Twenty-First Annual Meeting, December 1895 (Minneapolis, 1895), pp. 145-50.

[20]W.H. Maher, On the Road to Riches (Chicago, 1893), p. 87.

[21]Saunders Norvell, Forty Years of Hardware (New York: Hardware Age, 1924), p. 39.

[22]E.C. Simmons, "A Half Century in Hardware," Iron Age, January 4, 1906, p. 147.

[23]Norvell, op. cit., p. 92.

[24]Saint Louis Grocer, December 23, 1880, quoted in J. Nimmo, Jr., op. cit., p. 209, Appendix.

[25]E.C. Simmons, op. cit., p. 146.

[26]Chicago Tribune, Annual Review of the Trade and Commerce of the City of Chicago for the Year Ending December 31st, 1870 (Chicago, 1871), p. 59.

[27]William H. Ukers, "The Romance of Package Coffee," Nation's Business, July, 1923, pp. 40-2.

[28]S.H. Ditchett, Marshall Field and Company (New York: Dry Goods Economist, 1922), pp. 99-110.

[29]Melvin T. Copeland, op. cit., p. 601.

[30]Printers' Ink, June 15, 1889, p. 613.

[31]Norvell, op. cit., pp. 324-5.

[32] Printers' Ink, July 27, 1892, p. 92.

[33] From a survey of some of the journals in question.

[34] Printers' Ink, July 28, 1938, pp. 127-8.

[35] Ibid., p. 13.

[36] David Kinley, "Credit Instruments in Business Transactions," Journal of Political Economy, Vol. V, No. 2, March 1897, p. 161; Frederick B. Goddard, Giving and Getting Credit (New York: F. Tennyson Neely, 1896), p. 14; P.R. Earling, Whom To Trust: A Practical Treatise on Mercantile Credit (Chicago: Rand, McNally and Company, 1890), p. 18.

[37] Earling, op. cit., p. 236.

[38] Maher, op. cit., p. 65.

[39] Edward M. Skinner, "Credits and Collections in a Wholesale House," The Businessman's Library (Chicago: The System Company, 1907), Vol. I, p. 94.

[40] Ibid., pp. 92-3.

[41] Earling, op. cit., p. 301.

[42] Thomas F. Meagher, The Commercial Agency System of the United States and Canada Exposed (New York, 1876), William T. Chinn, The Mercantile Agencies Against Commerce (Chicago, 1896).

[43] Edward D. Page, "Single Name Commercial Paper under New Banking System--The Merchant's Viewpoint," Trust Companies, March, 1914, Number 3, p. 206. Quoted in Roy A. Foulke, The Sinews of American Commerce (New York: Dun and Bradstreet, 1941), p. 156.

[44] National Wholesale Druggists Association, Proceedings of Annual Meeting, September 2-5, 1895 (Minneapolis, 1895), pp. 130-1.

[45] Frederick B. Goddard, Giving and Getting Credit (New York: F. Tennyson Neely, 1896), p. 23.

[46] A History of the National Wholesale Druggists Association (New York: The Association, 1924), p. 50.

[47] Loc. cit.

[48]National Wholesale Druggists Association, Proceedings of the Twenty-Sixth Annual Meeting (Chicago, 1900), pp. 93-100.

[49]History of the National Wholesale Druggists Association, op. cit., p. 51.

[50]E.D. Page, "Lessons of the Claflin Crash," The Independent, July 13, 1914, p. 76.

[51]S.H. Ditchett, Marshall Field and Company (New York: Dry Goods Economist, 1922), Ch. XVII.

[52]National Wholesale Conference, Report of Committee I, Wholesalers' Functions and Services (Washington: Chamber of Commerce of the United States, reprinted, 1929), p. 19.

[53]United States Department of Commerce, Modernizing and Operating Grocery Warehouses (Washington: U.S. Government Printing Office, 1951), p. 1.

[54]United States Department of Commerce, Effective Use of Wholesale Drug Warehouses (Washington: U.S. Government Printing Office, 1947), p. 10.

[55]Ditchett, op. cit., p. 99.

[56]James E. Nichols, "The Grocery Trade," in One Hundred Years of American Commerce, C.M. Depew, Ed. (New York: D.O. Haynes and Co., 1895), p. 600.

[57]Norvell, op. cit., pp. 31-2.

[58]Norvell, op. cit., p. 315.

[59]Simmons, op. cit,. p. 146.

[60]See page 41 for discussion of the position of these middlemen in 1860.

[61]D.W. Sheldon, "Old Shipping Merchants of New York," Harper's Monthly, February, 1892, Vol. 84, p. 457.

[62]Boston Board of Trade, Twenty-Ninth Annual Report, 1882 (Boston, 1883), p. 60.

[63]Hunt's Merchant Magazine, 1860, Vol. 58, pp. 286-7.

[64]See page 41.

[65]Examples of these advertisements are common. See, for instance, Boston Directory, 1899; Baltimore Directory, 1899; St. Louis City Directory, 1887; Boston Board of Trade, Twenty-Ninth Annual Report, (Boston, 1883); Bradstreet's, September 29, 1880, p. 8.

[66]See also Paul T. Cherington, The Wool Industry (New York: A.W. Shaw Company, 1916), p. 136.

[67]Melvin T. Copeland, The Cotton Manufacturing Industry of the United States (Cambridge: Harvard University Press, 1917), p. 233.

[68]Norbert Savay, Principles of Foreign Trade (New York: The Ronal Press Company, 1919), p. 92.

[69]Final Report of the Industrial Commission (Washington: Government Printing Office, 1902), p. 580.

[70]U.S. House of Representatives, Report of the Commission upon the Best Modes of Securing More Intimate International and Commercial Relations Between the U.S. and Central American and South America (Washington: Government Printing Office, 1885), p. 15.

CHAPTER V

AGENT WHOLESALERS

The preceding chapter was concerned with the development of merchant wholesalers in the United States. The purpose of this chapter is to describe and analyze the changes which took place between 1860 and 1900 in the status and operations of another important class of middlemen, the agent wholesalers.

As previously indicated there is a basic distinction between these two groups of wholesalers.[1] The merchant wholesaler is a merchant middleman who sells, usually in fairly large quantities, to retailers and other merchants and/or to industrial, institutional and commercial users but who does not sell in significant amounts to ultimate consumers. In contrast to this are the agent wholesalers who negotiate purchases and/or sales but do not take title to the goods. The merchant wholesaler takes possession of the goods he handles but, depending upon the particular type of operation, the agent wholesalers may or may not take possession.

The differences between merchant and agent wholesalers are quite clear as are the distinctions between the various types of agent wholesalers. It is well to bear in mind, however, that business firms do not necessarily operate as one type of organization. This was particularly true during the period under consideration and especially with the agent wholesalers. The latter, like the merchant wholesalers, were in a state of transition and rapid development. It has been shown that it was not unusual in 1860 to find a single agent wholesaler operating in two or more agent capacities or combining agent and merchant functions. Although the trend subsequently was toward an every-increasing degree of functional specialization, this practice of combining two or more types of operations continued to some extent through 1900.

Nevertheless, the operations of most of the agent wholesalers fall into a pattern and can be described and analyzed as part of a class. Attention in the present discussion will be centered on auctioneers, commission merchants or factors, selling agents, merchandise brokers, and manufacturers' agents.

Auctions

Declining importance of auctions. Following 1860 the use of auction sales as outlets for manufactured goods decreased. Although the number of auctioneers in the United States increased up until 1890, their importance as wholesale middlemen decreased relatively and absolutely after the Civil War. The data by decades are as follows:[2]

	Number of auctioneers in the United States
1850	890
1860	1,348
1870	2,266
1880	2,331
1890	3,205
1900	2,808

The following schedule of duties, collected on sales at auction between 1860 and 1893 in the state of New York, illustrates their decline in one of the more important auction centers of the country.[3]

Year	Amount	Year	Amount
1860	$125,929.83	1877	$64,294.36
1861	75,318.33	1878	49,673.29
1862	77,358.57	1879	38,407.51
1863	108,604.67	1880	32,997.97
1864	154,425.86	1881	31,900.99
1865	195,608.65	1882	26,465.67
1866	269,720.23	1883	24,472.68
1867	191,618.67	1884	22,673.29
1868	127,701.72	1885	18,872.50
1869	95,785.64	1886	19,089.81
1870	121,602.18	1887	18,041.06
1871	100,196.88	1888	17,416.75
1872	79,069.96	1889	9,087.91
1873	76,499.37	1890	2,707.43
1874	69,756.59	1891	2,990.28
1875	70,432.05	1892	8,580.73
1876	75,788.00	1893	393.75

During the eighteen years 1860-77 the duties totaled $2,079,712.06 of which $2,077,537.29, or more than 99.8 percent, was paid by auctioneers residing in New York City and Brooklyn.[4] The temporary rise in the duties between 1863 and 1866 is probably attributable in part, first, to the rapid rise in wholesale prices during that time and, secondly perhaps, to increased activity resulting from the Civil War.[5] Third, a new agent had taken office in 1861 as collector of auction duties for the state and was apparently enforcing the law more vigorously than had his predecessor. In his report for 1865 the comptroller of New York said:

> The receipts from auction duties, during the year ending 30th September 1865, amounted to the sum of $195,608.65. There has been a large and steady increase in the revenue from this source, ever since the appointment of the present competent and faithful agent. The amount now reported, is considerably more than double that which was received four years ago.[6]

These duties were paid by the person making the sales and were calculated upon the amount for which the goods were sold. The items subject to duty included wines and ardent spirits, foreign and domestic, at the rate of one percent; East India goods, one-half of one percent; all other foreign goods three-quarters of one percent. These rates remained unchanged throughout the period for which auction duty receipts are shown above.[7]

Instances of decreases of auction sales in other areas could be cited but the preceding data seem to provide ample verification for the conclusion that between 1866 and 1900 auctions declined considerably in importance. Duties collected in New York fell from nearly $270,000 in 1866 to less than four hundred dollars in 1893, the last year in which the New York comptroller's reports show that duties were collected. It is true that the data presented above do not include sales at auction of domestic goods other than liquor; however, this does not invalidate the conclusion. Except for a brief period around 1830 the majority of merchandise sold at auction in New York was of foreign origin.[8] Thus, the evidence seems to indicate clearly that auctions declined in importance both absolutely and relatively during this period.

Volume of auction sales. The fact that auctions were declining during the period under consideration has been pointed out. The emphasis placed on this discussion should not be construed to mean, however, that this method of selling at wholesale was never utilized or that there were no lines of trade in which it was important during at least a part of the period. As a matter of fact, a number of instances of the use of auctions can be cited.

Philadelphia, for instance, was a city in which considerable quantities of goods were sold at auction. In 1881, a year of generally high business activity, the Board of Trade reported that:

> The wholesale auction houses have been kept pretty busy during the year, the offerings of goods, both foreign and domestic, being very large from this city, Baltimore, New York, and Boston. The boot and shoe sales have included full lines of all the different varieties of Philadelphia, New York, and New England manufacture. There appears to be a very marked increase in the quantity of Philadelphia made goods, of this line of business, selling at auction, apparently made for such purposes. The sales of dry goods, hosiery, and fancy goods have undoubtedly been much larger than usual, in consequence of the greatly increased activity of trade, caused by the universal prosperity, the superabundance of money, and the remarkable influence exerted upon the retail traffic by the immense exertions of various colossal establishments to advertise their wares and to attract customers on a great scale.[9]

In addition to sales of boots and shoes, dry goods, hosiery, and fancy goods mentioned in the preceding quotation numerous other items were being sold at auction in Philadelphia during this time. Considerable attention was being devoted to sales of objects of art, statuary, paintings, fine marble work, house ornaments, oriental goods, and fancy works.[10]

Also by this time there was a noticeable relative increase in the sale at auction of domestic goods compared to the value of foreign merchandise sold in this manner. The data on New York auction duties as well as the following quotation lend support to this conclusion:

> The sales of foreign merchandise of all kinds at our auction houses have increased during the past year in a marked degree, in consequence of the enormous enlargement of foreign importations at New York, where great stocks of manufactured goods from Europe arrive in immense masses, to be sold in any way and every way possible, so that for the purpose of rapid sale the Philadelphia auction houses are always valuable adjuncts. But in the last ten years domestic manufacturers of the New England and Middle States have very decidedly acquired the leading hand in all departments of the auction business, which leadership they show no disposition to part with, as the auction sales are largely managed in their interest, and find in the home manufacturers the very best contributors on a large scale to all their sales. Thus while the New England and New York manufacturers contribute largely to our auction sales, our own local manufacturers contribute enormously to the wholesale auctions of New York.[11]

This increase continued, the Board of Trade reporting in 1882 that the Philadelphia auctions were doing a large business in such merchandise as domestic dry goods, boots and shoes, rubber goods, tropical fruits, and groceries with a marked increase in quantities and values.[12]

In Boston auction sales seem to have reached a peak between 1850 and 1860 declining thereafter. In a review of fifty years of Boston commerce it was reported in 1882 that:

> The commercial auction sales of Boston in those days presented a feature not to be easily forgotten by those who were participants...The auction sales of Boston 1850 to 1860, were as distinguishing a feature as her public institutions.[13]

Auctions were, of course, used as a method of sale at wholesale market centers and lines of trade other than those already mentioned.

Another line in which the auction method of sale was assuming some importance during this period was fruit and produce although major developments in this field apparently took place after 1900.[14] Before that time, however, there was, for example, a fruit auction company operating in Cincinnati:

> A few fruit commission houses have formed a fruit auction company. Sales of lemons, oranges, and pineapples are made through this channel to an important extent. The plan of operation is this: Each firm belonging to the fruit auction company sends all consigned fruit to them to be sold on commission to the fruit auctions. The sales are advertised to take place at a certain time. Samples of fruit are displayed and sales are made to the highest bidder. In this manner it is easy to keep the supplies from becoming burdensome, and all members of the fruit auction company are in a position to know how receipts and demand are running. There are two of these fruit auctions in operation.[15]

Quantities of goods were also sold at auction in such lines as flannels, blankets and carpets but these appear to have been declining rapidly in importance during this period.[16] For instance, auctions were not uncommon in the sale of carpets prior to 1870 but subsequently disappeared except for occasional use to dispose of excess inventories.[17] Even before 1860 it was said of the trade in woolens that, "in Boston, the auction business is reduced in a greater ratio than in this [New York] city. In Philadelphia there has also been a falling off. In Baltimore it amounts to nothing as compared with private sales."[18]

Occasional notices or announcements of auctions in these and other lines of trade can be found but the auction cannot be said to have represented a regularly employed method of distribution after the Civil War.

Reasons for the decline. The diminishing importance of auctions following the Civil War was an extension of the trend in this direction which was apparent in 1860.[19] The same factors continued to influence auctions adversely and were responsible for their decreasing significance as institutions in wholesaling.

Large proportions of the merchandise sold at auction were dry goods. Even before 1860 textile selling agents were becoming important in the distribution of these products. Textiles were diverted from the auctions to the selling agents. These agents sold to the retailers who, in many cases, had been accustomed to visit the central markets and buy their needs at auction.

As transportation and communication facilities were improved, foreign sellers took advantage of the possibilities to contact wholesalers in the United States directly. Instead of buying at auction the wholesale middlemen purchased directly thus bypassing the auction and contributing to its decline.

The growth of other marketing institutions, particularly the brokers described below, and the rise of interior market centers discussed in Chapter III, were also factors important in accelerating the trend away from the use of auctions. The comptroller of the state of New York said in 1863 that:

> A large proportion of the foreign goods which alone are subject to these duties are sold by a class of brokers for the purpose of avoiding the payment to which they would be liable if sold at auction. The revenue from this source would undoubtedly be increased very largely by subjecting these brokers' sales to the same duties as the auction sales. It is but simple justice to require the same payment from one class as from the other.[20]

If the comptroller's statement is true that revenue would have been increased "very largely" by assessing brokers the same as auctions, and there is little reason to doubt it, then it must be concluded that by 1863 there was a considerable diversion of trade from the auctions to brokers. This was the case not only with foreign goods but also with domestic merchandise.

These brokers and other wholesalers were developing rapidly in the interior as well as in the coastal centers. Merchants who had made it a practice to travel to the central markets and buy at

auction were now solicited at their places of business by traveling
representatives of these wholesalers. Some of the auctioneers in New
York in 1880 specifically attributed the decline in their business to
the development of traveling salesmen. This development made it
uneconomical for the retailer to visit the auctions.[21] It was also
possible for the country merchant to visit the interior markets,
where auctions had never become so important as in the eastern
centers, and buy direct from the wholesalers there.

Credit seems to have been a constant problem for the retailer
and he preferred to buy where long terms were available. The
auctions did not satisfy this requirement. Attempts were made by the
auction companies, in some instances, to sell on credit. It was
reported of the Philadelphia furniture trade in 1880 that:

> The auction houses are extensively used to
> supply the retail trade, and many firms sell
> goods on the installment plan, and altogether, in
> the course of the year regular consumption of
> this cheap furniture by the city trade is very
> large.[22]

This practice was apparently neither very successful nor
widespread for little mention of it is made elsewhere in the
literature.

Thus, although considerable quantities of goods were sold at
auction at various times this method of sale was diminishing in
importance in most trade for the reasons mentioned.

Commission Merchants

Another class of agent middlemen who experienced a considerable evolutionary change between 1860 and 1900 were the commission merchants, or factors.

Commission merchants defined. A commission merchant is an agent who receives goods on consignment and sells them on commission. He has physical control of but not title to the goods and may transact such business in his own name. During the period in question these middlemen were defined as follows:

> A factor or commission merchant may be defined as an agent employed to purchase or sell goods on commission, either in his own name or the name of his principal; and he is intrusted with the possession, management, control and disposal of the goods bought or sold. A commission merchant is a factor. The common law once distinguished factors, or commission merchants, as either home or foreign, which classification was determined by the residence of the principal. This distinction does not apply with us, when the principal is domiciled in one of the United States and his factor in another.[23]

As a matter of fact, the terms commission merchant and factor had become synonymous even before 1860. Foulke points out that they had become "quite synonymous" by the second quarter of the nineteenth century although the factor probably was more representative of the firm that handled imported merchandise.[24] Hill pointed out in 1879 that the terms factor and commission merchant could be used interchangeably but that the factor is "the agent of a merchant living abroad."[25]

The word factor fell into disuse during this period except in cotton and naval stores with reference to factoring of accounts receivable. This was a special usage and will be discussed later. In 1884 it was pointed out that:

> The term 'factor' has become practically obsolete, not only on the floor of the Exchange, but in the general vernacularism of the country. Therefore, we shall hereafter, use the word 'commission merchant', as being fully synonymous, in contemplation of the law, with what has been habitually expressed by the term 'factor'. And besides, what has heretofore been described as a factor, answers to what has been for sometime known as a commission merchant or consignee for sale.[26]

Commission merchant declining in relative importance. What information is available seems to indicate that the commission merchant was declining in relative importance during the period under consideration. There are no census data on which to base such a conclusion but other sources indicate that it is correct. For example, in reviewing the previous twenty years in the wool trade the secretary of the National Association of Wool Manufacturers said in 1879 that:

> Besides these improvements in the mills, there have been improvements in the system of business and manufacture. There has been a greater independence of the commission merchant, manufacturers more generally selling their own goods. The intervention of jobbers in medium and low priced goods has to a large degree disappeared through the large sale of goods directly to the most important consumers, the clothing manufacturers, causing a more rigid inspection of goods at the mill from having skilled buyers, and insuring greater perfection,

> thus fulfilling the law of political economy,
> that the customer and producer should be brought
> as nearly as possible together.27

Although commission merchants were important in the sale of
cotton the same decline appears to have been taking place there as in
wool:

> With the increasing number of cotton
> factories in the South a larger amount of cotton
> is being sold directly to the mills. If it could
> be grown without the advances these charges might
> all be saved. But the party [factors] making
> advances stipulates that such a number of bales
> be brought to them for storage and sale, and in
> case the specified number is not delivered a
> forfeit of $1.50 for each bale short of the
> number is to be paid. The transactions of the
> farmer with the factory are very satisfactory.
> The morning paper informs both parties of the
> price of cotton the world over. The farmer is
> the better for saving the charges of the factor,
> and the mill saves agents' charges for buying,
> drayage, and freight, so that they agree easily
> with one another.28

The industrial commission concluded that between 1875 and 1900
there was a constant tendency to reduce the difference between what
the consumer paid for farm products and the producer received. A
large part of this reduction in cost of marketing, it said, was due
to reduction in risk. It is pointed out in the report that after
1885 rates of commission were reduced so much that, "the old style
commission business has been doomed to disappear in the cotton and
the grain trades, the hay trade, and, to a considerable extent, in
many other kinds of distribution.29

The Commission further stated that the "probability is, however,
that the entire business of selling on commission is antiquated and

should have been abandoned long ago. In various lines of trade in farm products it is beginning to disappear or has disappeared, much to the satisfaction of all concerned.[30]

Commission merchants handling large volumes in some lines. Although it is true that commission merchants were declining in importance there were still a number of lines in which they constituted a vital part of the distribution machinery. During the period in question they were handling quantities of such commodities as cotton, wool, livestock, tobacco, textiles, and grain, to name a few. As a matter of fact they are still important today in the sale of livestock and grain and also handle textiles, naval stores, and fruit and vegetables.[31]

That there were still other lines in which commission merchants functioned is indicated by the following statement concerning trade in Cincinnati in 1873:

> In the dry goods field the middle-men, or
> commission merchants, have more than maintained
> their position. There has been a decided
> increase in the quantity of goods sold by this
> class. Business too, has been conducted in the
> presence of fewer obstacles...The whole business
> has stood more nearly upon its actual merits,
> than ever before. There certainly is no reason
> why, if sheetings, jeans, and satinets, and flan-
> nels, and other articles upon which our domestic
> manufacturers have expended their attention, are
> sold, relatively, as low here as in New York,
> that the purchase should not be made here.[32]

In Cincinnati in that year there were commission merchants representing 63 cotton mills and 85 woolen mills from practically every producing state in the union.

Numerous other instances of the operation of commission
merchants could be cited. The following is interesting, by way of
example, of the part commission merchants were playing in the
marketing of cattle by 1900:

> From southwestern sources cattle are
> marketed through commission merchants at market
> centers under favorable conditions to all parties
> concerned. There is also the local buyer, whose
> purchases from the grower ultimately pass into
> the commission merchants' hands. There are,
> therefore, at the utmost three persons through
> whose hands the cattle pass from the ranch to the
> packer: the local dealer, the railroad, and the
> commission merchant. The rate of commission at
> most large markets is 50 cents per head. The
> rise of the mammoth slaughter house
> establishments has brought into the productive
> territory the buyers for these houses. This, of
> course, eliminates all other commercial expenses
> except the salary of the buyer and freight.[33]

Specialization by commission merchants. There seems to have
been less specialization by products among commission merchants
between 1860 and 1900 than among some of the other types of agent
middlemen. An examination of the directories of some of the
principal wholesale markets and of the membership lists of the
various boards of trade indicate that during this period there were
commission merchants who specialized in the following:[34]

Brewer's supplies	Grain and hay
Carpets	Grain and provisions
Cotton	Hardware
Dry goods	Iron
Fancy goods	Livestock
Fish	Lumber
Flour	Lumber and plaster
Fruit	Oils
Grain	Produce
Grain and flour	Seed

Tobacco   Wool
Whisky   Woolens

As indicated earlier the combination of various types of
wholesaling operations was not uncommon with the commission merchant
in 1860. This continued to be the case throughout the remainder of
the 19th century. Many advertised themselves as doing a shipping and
commission business. The combination of forwarding and commission
was not so common by 1900 as it had been in 1860 for reasons
mentioned in Chapter II. The agent-merchant type of operation is
described by Thompson in discussing the situation in the distribution
of produce prior to 1900:

> While a considerable number of produce men
> who began buying on a commission basis took up
> jobbing later, it was not uncommon to find a
> combination of both methods employed by the same
> firm. Dealers might handle certain lines on a
> commission and buy other produce outright. Again
> a given commodity might be bought and sold in job
> lots at certain times and be taken in only on a
> commission basis later under different
> conditions. Such combinations of commission and
> jobbing business are still a common practice in
> all our leading trade centers.[35]

This practice by commission merchants of carrying on a combined
type of operation accounts in large part for the lack of good
quantitative data about this class of middlemen.

Another aspect of this same point is that of functional
specialization by some commission merchants which took place first
primarily among those who dealt in imported goods and textiles. The
selling function of these agents was gradually discontinued and they
became specialized banking institutions for the textile industry.

These operations were subsequently extended to include such other products as men's clothing, furniture and shoes.[36]

As has been shown the terms factor and commission merchant were synonymous but the use of the term "factor" to mean commission merchant declined. By 1900 it was most commonly used in referring to agents who performed a specialized banking function for their principals. This is the special usage of the term which was mentioned earlier.

The factor discounted accounts receivable and made loans against merchandise to his principal. One authority describes the change which took place as follows:

> Between 1889 and 1905 the factoring business underwent a radical change. The selling function was gradually discontinued and the factor became a specialized banking institution for the textile industry...He continued to perform all the other services. Before an order for merchandise was filled, the order would be turned over to the factor who would decide if the buyer was or was not financially responsible. If responsible, the factor would guarantee the payment of the account to the mill making the sales and at monthly intervals would buy these receivables outright from the mill without recourse. Advances of funds would also be made, as from time immemorial, against merchandise.[37]

These factors devoted most of their attention to the handling of the business of foreign sellers of textiles. The passage of the McKinley tariff act of 1890, however, raised the duties on foreign textiles to such an extent that it was practically impossible for them to compete in American markets. This caused the factor to turn his attention to domestic producers and sellers but the American mills preferred to retain their own sales departments. Thus the selling function of the factor tended to disappear and he became instead a banker, discounting receivables and advancing credit to domestic sellers. This evolution had been largely completed by 1905.[38]

Reasons for the declining importance of commission merchants. Enough evidence has been introduced to support the conclusion that, although they were handling large quantities of goods, commission merchants declined in importance in many lines of trade between 1860 and 1900. There were several reasons for this.

In the first place commission merchants were severely criticized for lack of honesty in their dealings with principals. The principal and agent were often far enough separated that it was not difficult for the latter to falsify his reports of prices received and expenses incurred. Furthermore, the commission merchants were accused of selling to themselves when it was profitable to do so and to others when it was unprofitable to buy, thus making profits and commission in the first instance and commissions in the second.[39]

There is no way in which to determine the honesty, or lack of honesty, of the commission merchant during this period. Probably they were little more unscrupulous than other classes of businessmen. The actual facts of the case do not matter; the point is that the seller's attitude toward these middlemen was, in many instances, one of distrust. It is probable this situation contributed to the

decreasing importance of commission merchants.

In discussing the city distribution of farm products Urner

points out that in 1880 most of the wholesale receivers of domestic

produce in the city markets were commission merchants. They did

business purely on an agency basis, the charge for selling wholesale

lots to jobbers ranging from ten percent for fruit and vegetables

down to five percent for butter, cheese, eggs, and poultry.[40] He

states that under the stresses of competition the lines of

demarcation between wholesale receivers and jobbers were tending

toward obliteration. This movement began prior to 1900 and continued

thereafter:

> Jobbers, in the effort to obtain supplies
> more cheaply, have reached out to primary sources
> of supply, over the heads of the wholesale
> receivers; and the latter, in order to maintain
> their hold upon supplies, have reached out over
> the heads of jobbers for outlets to retailers, so
> that the two classes of trade formerly distinct
> have tended toward unification. But in respect
> to a large part of the farm products, especially
> such as are of the most perishable nature, this
> more direct movement has not yet become possible,
> and at the present time we find in the large
> markets not only commission merchants and jobbers
> but also many wholesalers who perform both
> functions, and many who besides acting as agents
> for some producers and shippers deal also in
> products for their own account.[41]

It seems logical to conclude that the reason why the commission

merchant preceded the wholesale merchant as an important distributor

of farm products was the risk involved in the operations. As

producers learned systematic methods of packing, as handling was improved and transportation speeded up, the produce reached the market in a more salable condition. Thus receivers began to handle these items on a merchant basis as it became progressively less hazardous to assume responsibility for their quality, safety, and salability in the market. Outright sale rather than consignment selling appealed to the producers and shippers.

It is probably that the behavior of prices during the latter part of the period, 1860 to 1900, was not particularly influential in bringing about the change. A period of constant or rising prices would encourage middlemen to buy outright for resale rather than to handle goods on consignment and a falling price level would tend to have the opposite effect. Of course, the reverse would probably be true for shippers. It is true that this was a period of falling prices generally; however, particularly after about 1886, fluctuations were not violent and after 1895 prices began to rise.[42] Thus, if the price situation did not contribute positively to the increasing relative importance of merchant operations in the handling of farm products neither did it present a serious obstacle to this development. The rate of price decline was comparatively moderate and there were several short periods during which prices were fairly constant.

Selling Agents

Before 1860 some commission merchants began specializing in textiles and from these evolved the selling agents. These are agents who operate on an extended contractual basis selling all of the output in a given line of one or more producers. They generally have full authority regarding prices and terms of sale and may help in financing the principal.[43]

Several conditions favored the growth of selling agents. When the manufacturers were small and did not have an intimate acquaintance with the market the selling agents proved to be a good outlet for their products. Furthermore, the agents were in a position to provide financial aid to the mills who were often financially weak. This was particularly important in view of the long credits which prevailed in the nineteenth century. Thus the selling agents could and did perform two essential functions for their principals, those of selling and financing.

As a matter of fact, the selling agent sometimes bought the mills. Cherington states that:

> While many of the early selling houses were concerned mainly with cotton mills, the woolen and worsted mills followed the same historical course, often operating and being owned side by side with cotton mills under a single selling house.[44]

Thus, in 1860 the textile manufacturers customarily sold their output through these specialized commission merchants, known generally in the textile trade as selling agents.

After the Civil War, however, the business climate became less favorable for the selling agents. This was especially true in the North and subsequently also in the South. Manufacturers were

becoming larger and financially stronger and this tended to make them
less dependent upon their selling agents for financial aid. The lack
of capital had been fully as influential as any other consideration
in causing some of the mills to rely on selling agents.[45] In
addition, improvements in transportation and communications brought
the mill into closer contact with its markets, further obviating the
necessity of the use of selling agents. Still another factor working
against the selling agent was competition. Competitive pressures
exerted a downward influence on prices and manufacturers were anxious
to lower costs to avoid being caught in a squeeze. This they
attempted to do by eliminating or absorbing their selling houses.

Briefly, then, those were the influences which tended to bring
about a decline in importance of the selling agent and favored sale
through brokers or direct selling by the manufacturers. There is
ample evidence to indicate that such a change did take place before
1900. For example, an 1895 report on the wool trade stated that:

> The commission business grew with the growth
> of the mills, and the two lines of business
> became so intimately associated and blended
> through joint ownership that the points of
> demarcation were almost indistinguishable. There
> were advantages and disadvantages connected with
> this relationship; but the lesson of experience
> has been that the manufacturer has not as a whole
> been the gainer from it; that it is a
> relationship peculiar to the formative period of
> industrial development and necessitated rather by
> limited capital than by inherent fitness. In the
> evolution of later years, emphasized by the harsh
> experiences of manufacturers in time of
> commercial crisis, the tendency has been steadily
> towards the independence of the producer in the
> direction of the selling of his own goods.[46]

A similar example of this change comes from the dry goods trade of which it was reported in 1890 that:

> In manufactures of cotton, whilst prices ruled higher than last year, the cost of raw materials told against producers, and although agents, commission houses and jobbers made in the aggregate a larger distribution of goods than in the average of recent years, their returns suffered from the gradual increase of expenses attendant upon more costly styles of doing business. Manufacturers have had to face the same thing, and a feature of the year was the increasing number of them, who, dispensing with agents and commission houses, entered the market as sellers of their own productions.[47]

Between 1870 and 1890 there was an increase in the use of sales agents in the carpet trade coincident with a decrease in importance of the commission house. Here also, the sales agent provided financial and merchandising assistance as well as handling the sale of the product. In view of the increasing complexities and difficulties of selling during this time this appealed to the manufacturers.[48]

However, after 1890 there was also in the carpet trade a tendency on the part of manufacturers to dispense with the selling agent and to sell directly to the trade through their own salesmen.[49] This practice was undertaken by a number of companies, apparently in an effort to increase their incomes by taking over the wholesaling functions.

Although it is clear that there was an effort on the part of manufacturers to dispense with the selling agent, it should not be inferred that the latter was entirely eliminated. There were still small manufacturers who needed sales and financial assistance and there were selling agents handling numerous accounts and doing large volumes. For example, the Cone Export and Commission Company represented, at the time it was established in 1891, thirty-eight southern plaid mills. These mills had agreed to sell their output exclusively through Cone for five years.[50]

As indicated the selling agents declined less rapidly in the South than in the North. They were important in the development of southern textile mills between 1880 and 1910.

Merchandise Brokers

Brokers defined. The broker is an agent middleman who represents either buyer or seller and does business for his principals. He does not have physical control of the goods and his power as to prices and terms are usually limited by his principal. This is a currently employed definition and apparently has changed but little since before 1900. For example, in 1879 the law defined a broker as:

> An agent employed to make bargains and
> contracts between other persons in matters of
> trade, for a compensation commonly called
> brokerage, or more recently, commissions; in
> other words a broker is one who makes a bargain
> for another and receives a commission for so
> doing. He is a mere negotiator between other
> parties, and never acts in his own name, but in
> the name of those who employ him. When he is
> employed to buy or sell goods, he is not
> authorized to buy or sell them in his own name.
> He is a middleman and for some purposes is
> treated as an agent of both parties. Where he is
> employed to buy and sell goods, it is the custom
> to give the buyer a note of the sale, called a

> sold note, and to the seller a like note called a
> bought note, in his own name, as agent of each,
> whereby they are respectively bound, if he has
> not exceeded his authority.[51]

This definition includes all types of brokers such as exchange, real estate, stock, ship, and merchandise brokers. The present discussion is centered on the latter class, those engaged in effecting the purchase and sale of merchandise.

Importance of brokers as wholesale distributors. Some of the same factors contributing to the decline of the auction method of selling were benefiting merchandise brokers. The latter were an integral part of the distribution system by 1860 and continued thereafter to increase in importance. By 1900 merchandise brokers were common in the marketing channels of a wide range of lines. The following is a list of some of these trades. In spite of its length it should probably be interpreted as suggestive rather than all-inclusive:[52]

Cattle	Lumber
Chemicals	Metal
China and India goods	Molasses
Coffee	Oil
Cotton	Paints and colors
Cotton goods	Produce
Drugs	Provisions
Dry goods	Rice
Dye stuffs	Rubber
Flour	Silk
Fruits and spices	Spices
Grain	Starch
Hay	Sugar
Hemp	Tea
Hides and leather	Tin
Horses	Tobacco
Iron	Wines and liquor
Lard	Wool

Brokers seem to have been particularly important in the
distribution of such commodities as livestock, cotton, grain, and
wool. There is little statistical data available before 1900
concerning the number of merchandise brokers operating in the various
lines. In 1882, however, the Boston Board of Trade reported that:

> The Wool Trade of Boston, as a distinct
> branch, is of comparatively recent date, and yet,
> within thirty years, it has assumed gigantic
> proportions, and comes well up among the millions
> annually returned to the statistical bureau.
> Fifty years ago the firm of Livermore and
> Kendall, the parent firm of Morse, Denny and Co.,
> opened Quincy Hall as a Wool house, the first of
> the kind, in this city, as a distinct branch of
> commerce...

> In 1841, there were 2 dealers and 1 broker.
> " 1851,   "   "   12   "   "   2 brokers.
> " 1861,   "   "   7   "   "   3   "
> " 1867,   "   "   18   "   "   5   "
> " 1879,   "   "   44   "   " 42   "
> " 1881,   "   "   48   "   " 42   "

> These figures represent only establishments that
> were dealing exclusively in Wool.[53]

Merchandise brokers were also important in the distribution of
cotton. The investigations of the Industrial Commission in 1900
showed that brokers were operating in most of the cotton marketing
centers by that time.[54] Some indication of the cotton broker's
efficiency is contained in the Commission's conclusion that at that
time the cotton producer came nearer getting the consumers' price for
his cotton than did the producers of any other important agricultural
commodity.

A part of the reason for the larger share of the consumers'
dollar going to cotton producers than was the case in other trades
may have been due to differences in physical handling and
transportation costs. Nevertheless, it appears to be a safe
conclusion that by 1900, at least, the cotton broker was an
economical means of distribution:

> The tendency at the present time is
> everywhere to cut out the middleman. The
> depression of earlier years like all other
> depressions, while not finding an adequate remedy
> for itself at the time gradually worked
> revolutionary changes by eliminating commercial
> agencies and commercial methods which do not have
> in themselves the capacity to adopt economies
> such as enable commerce to recover from the
> paralysis of industrial depression. The exact
> cost of putting down cotton at foreign mills
> varies of course with localities, but on an
> average cotton can go from plantation to mill in
> Europe at the cost of about one cent per pound.
> Expenses have been greatly reduced in the export
> trade by more direct commercial relation between
> foreign consumers and local brokers. Brokers now
> operate in every town receiving any quantity of
> cotton. These brokers have correspondent brokers
> all over Europe through whom they sell to
> spinners direct, so that cotton can go from
> Augusta, Ga., for instance to any mill in England
> or on the Continent with only freight, insurance,
> and two small brokerages of one-sixteenth of a
> cent each covering all expenses.[55]

The foregoing quotation demonstrates the importance of brokers
in the sale of American cotton to foreign mills. This becomes even
more impressive when it is remembered that at this time approximately
seventy percent of the cotton raised in the United States was
exported. Moreover, brokers also figured in the distribution of
cotton within this country:

> Owing largely to the increase of banking
> facilities in the South and the lien law, which
> changed the relation of the farmer or renter from
> dealing with the cotton factor to dealing with
> the merchant, the crop has been sold more and
> more in the interior and at local markets and
> direct either to exporters or to brokers, who in
> turn sold to New England mills.[56]

One of the reasons for the declining importance of the cotton
factor, or commission merchant, was the increasing amount of interior
buying, usually done through brokers.[57] The extension of transportation and communication lines throughout the South after the Civil War
facilitated this development. Some of the mills in England and New
England began to send their own buying agents to the South but:

> Usually they have preferred to make use of
> that great class of nineteenth century traders,
> the brokers. The mill treasurer 'has now only to
> put a few packages of cotton outside his door,
> thereby indicating that he is buying, to receive
> calls from a great number of persons anxious to
> provide him with material.' These men are called
> 'buyers,' but they are in reality brokers.
> Having named the prices at which they can deliver
> cotton to the manufacturer, which they are able
> to do because the telegraph has put them into
> easy communication with all points in the South,
> and having received their orders, the brokers
> immediately telegraph to one of their agents
> among the brokers who are scattered throughout
> the South. These southern brokers go to the
> country merchants, or may even buy from the
> planter the cotton which he has brought to
> market.[58]

This use of brokers was advantageous to the buyers, the
manufacturers, as well as to the sellers, the country merchants or
planters. To the former there was a saving in transportation and
commission because cotton was moved from the interior direct to the

mill rather than going through the hands of the factors at the ports. The usual brokerage charge was fifty cents a bale. For the seller this method furnished a buyer who could pay cash for his purchases.[59]

As to the total number of brokers in the various trades in the United States no accurate data are available. From 1880 the decennial census reports classify brokers into two categories, commercial and stock brokers. In 1880 the number of commercial brokers was reported at 4,193; in 1890, 5,960; and in 1900 there were 7,334. By 1910 the census reported 24,009 commercial brokers and commission men and 8,664 brokers not specified.

In general, merchandise brokers appear to have been most active in the distribution of primary materials of which cotton and wool discussed above are exemplary. They also operated, however, in the marketing of manufactured goods and were especially active in the food trade. The early food brokers fitted the definition of the term broker given above. They located buyers for the products of the canneries and factories and they sought out sources of supply for the wholesalers.[60] The refinements in the 1860's of the techniques for commercial canning and preserving of food gave particular impetus to the development of these brokers who have come to be selling agents even though they are still referred to as brokers.[61]

Instances of the operation of brokers in other lines might be presented but the foregoing is sufficient to confirm and illustrate the conclusion that the number of brokers in the United States increased rapidly after 1860; that by 1900 they occupied an important place as specialists in the marketing of many lines of goods. The major reason for their growth was that they provided an economical means of distribution. Merchandise brokers were, and are, particularly valuable to the small producers, those who sell a limited line, and sellers of seasonal items. They provided a ready-made sales organization making it possible for the seller to predetermine his selling expenses. Because of their knowledge of the markets the brokers also rendered a valuable service to buyers in locating sources of supply. The rapid expansion of the markets between 1860 and 1900 provided a business climate favoring the development of brokers.

Manufacturers' Agents

Still another group of agent middlemen in wholesale trade were those known as manufacturers' agents. The term manufacturers' agent appeared occasionally in the literature in 1860 but apparently was used rather loosely, as was much of the terminology at this time, and was not used as we understand it today. In fact, Weld pointed out in 1917 that the lines of demarcation between brokers and manufacturers' agents in the grocery trade were rather indistinct at times.[62]

These middlemen are commonly defined as agents who sell part of the output of their manufacturer principals on an extended contractual basis. They usually represent two or more manufacturers of non-competing lines and have exclusive rights in the sale of those products in given territories. They are limited with respect to prices and terms of sale.

The manufacturers' agent arose to serve the small producer. Many manufacturers began business on a small scale. They lacked knowledge of the markets and the ability to sell so the manufacturers' agent fulfilled a real need for this class. This seems to have been particularly true of the grocery trade, although as sales increased manufacturers tended toward the operation of their own sales forces.[63] One manufacturers' agent handling food items reported that throughout his history he has been taking on accounts for newly advertised specialties only sometimes ultimately to lose the account after the product had become well established in the market.[64] This, of course, is not unusual but seems to be simply an occupational hazard among manufacturers' agents and is still the case today.[65]

Besides the grocery trade, manufacturers' agents were also of some importance by 1900 in the hardware trade. Many producers in this trade turned out only one or a few items and because he combined the output of several sellers the manufacturers' agent could perform the sales function economically. Weld concluded in 1917 that at that time there appeared to be no pronounced tendency in the hardware trade for the manufacturers' agents to become less important.[66]

Few of the directories before 1875 listed manufacturers' agents in their business classifications. After that time, however, they began to appear in increasing numbers. The St. Louis directory of 1884, for example, contained the names of 99 individuals and firms classified as manufacturers' agents. One was listed as handling machinery which is one of the lines in which these agents are numerous today. By 1900 the business directories in practically all the important wholesale centers contained numerous entries under this classification.

Summary

Those are the main features in the development of agent wholesalers operating between 1860 and 1900. The problem of precisely classifying all the various types of agent wholesalers is a difficult one because of the diversity of their operations. There are innumerable details and individual variations which could be described fully only in a long series of individual case studies. These variations are the result of historical, personal and competitive forces which have been exerted upon the wholesale structure through the years.

Nevertheless, a number of things are clear concerning the period under consideration and certain generalizations can be made. During this time auctioneers appear to have been more numerous than ever before but as wholesale distributors they were declining in importance. There were a number of reasons for this. Auctions had been used largely for the sale of foreign goods and these were declining in relative importance. Selling agents began to handle many of the goods which had formerly been sold at auction and auctioneers themselves were complaining that brokers were responsible for declines in their volume of sales. With the shift to a buyers' market competition became more severe and auctions were not equipped to cope with the new problems which arose. It was cheaper for merchants to buy at home from traveling salesmen than to travel to the central markets to attend auctions.

Commission merchants were handling quantities of goods but, like the auctioneers, they appear to have been decreasing in relative importance. Often the business of a commission merchant was combined with that of a merchant wholesaler and the stresses of competition were tending to dull the line of demarcation between these two types of operations. Improved methods of packing and grading and the extension of the lines of transportation and communication tended to enhance the importance of merchant operations. Commission merchants could not offer as efficient service as some of the more specialized middlemen. In some cases producers preferred to sell direct or through brokers, thus eliminating the commission merchant.

Selling agents were particularly important in the sale of textiles. They performed two important functions for their principals, those of financing and selling. They were important in the development of southern textiles even in the latter part of this period because they assumed the burdens of these functions often providing, in addition, valuable merchandising assistance. This left the manufacturers free to look after production. Following the Civil War there was a tendency for the larger manufacturers to abandon this method of sale and to perform their own selling functions.

By 1900 merchandise brokers were common in the distribution of a wide range of lines. They seem to have been most important, however, in the sale of such commodities as livestock, cotton, grain and wool as well as in manufactured goods. The evidence indicates that brokers were able to operate economically and this, along with the other reasons presented, accounts largely for their rapid growth during the period in question. There was more specialization among brokers than among commission merchants, for example, which may have been a further reason for the rise of the former and the decline of the latter.

Manufacturers' agents, a particular kind of broker, appear to have been less important during this period although they were operating in a number of trades by 1900. Probably the major reason for their rise was the fact that they combined the output of a number of different producers with consequent reductions in selling costs for any one.

On the basis of the foregoing a valid conclusion would seem to be that, in general, the rapid expansion of the markets during this period accounts for the importance of agent wholesalers, the more specialized increasing in importance while the less specialized declined.

FOOTNOTES - CHAPTER V

[1]See page 5.

[2]Twelfth Census, 1900, Occupations at the Twelfth Census, pp. xxxvixl.

[3]Annual Report of the Comptroller of the State of New York (Albany, 1861-1894).

[4]Documents of the Assembly of the State of New York (Albany, 1878), Vol. V, No. 64, p. 1.

[5]See chart of wholesale prices page 62.

[6]Annual Report of the Comptroller of the State of New York (Albany, 1866), p. 29.

[7]Cf. Report of the Comptroller of the State of New York, 1893, pp. 32-3, and the Comptroller's report, 1849, pp. 87-9.

[8]Fred M. Jones, "Middlemen in the Domestic Trade of the United States, 1800-1860," Illinois Studies in the Social Sciences, Vol. 21:3 (May, 1937), p. 33.

[9]Philadelphia Board of Trade, Forty-Eighth Annual Report (Philadelphia, 1881), pp. 119-20.

[10]Loc. cit.

[11]Op. cit., pp. 120-1.

[12]Philadelphia Board of Trade, Forty-Ninth Annual Report (Philadelphia, 1882), p. 112.

[13]Boston Board of Trade, Twenty-Ninth Annual Report (Boston, 1883), p. 39.

[14]Edwin G. Nourse, The Chicago Produce Market (Boston: Houghton Mifflin Company, 1918), pp. 32-8.

[15]Report of the Industrial Commission, Distribution of Farm Products (Washington, 1901), Vol. VI, p. 338.

[16]New York Chamber of Commerce, Thirty-Second Annual Report (New York, 1889), Part II, p. 87.

[17]An exception to this was the Alexander Smith Company which sold a part of its output at auction between 1900 and 1929. See A.H. Cole, The American Carpet Manufacture (Cambridge: Harvard University Press, 1941), pp. 202, 212.

[18]Documents of the Assembly of the State of New York (Albany, 1849), No. 218.

[19]See page 43.

[20]Annual Report of the Comptroller of the State of New York (Albany, 1863), p. 44.

[21]Chamber of Commerce of New York, Twenty-Third Annual Report (New York, 1881), Part II, p. 60.

[22]Philadelphia Board of Trade, Forty-Seventh Annual Report (Philadelphia, 1880), p. 118.

[23]L.H. Hisbee and J.C. Simonds, Law of the Produce Exchange (Chicago: Callaghan & Company, 1884), p. 134, citing Edwards on Factors and Brokers, Sec. 1; Russell on Mercantile Agency, p. 1; Buckley v. Packard, 20 John. 442; Duguid v. Edwards, 50 Barb. 288; L. Bell Comm. on Mer. Jur., 386, and Chitty on Com. and Man. 193-4.

[24]Roy A. Foulke, The Sinews of American Commerce (New York: Dun and Bradstreet, Inc., 1941), p. 186.

[25]Edward J. Hill, The Law of Commission (Chicago, 1879), pp. 7-8.

[26]Hisbee and Simonds, op. cit., pp. 142-3.

[27]Bulletin of the National Association of Wool Manufacturers (Boston, 1879), Vol. IX, p. 281.

[28]Report of the Industrial Commission, op. cit., p. 167.

[29]Ibid., p. 6.

[30]Ibid, p. 7.

[31]P.D. Converse, H.W. Huegy and R.V. Mitchell, The Elements of Marketing (New York: Prentice-Hall, Inc., 1952), p. 263.

[32]Cincinnati Chamber of Commerce, Twenty-Fifth Annual Report (Cincinnati, 1873), p. 86.

[33]Report of the Industrial Commission, op. cit., p. 250.

[34]Cf. similar list for 1860, page 42. Sources of this data were: Boston Directory, 1899; Baltimore Directory, 1899; Trow's Business Directory of Greater New York, 1906; Membership lists in Cincinnati Chamber of Commerce, Fifty-Second Annual Report, 1900; Chicago Board of Trade, Forty-Third Annual Report, 1900; Philadelphia Board of Trade, Sixty-Seventh Annual Report, 1900.

[35]C.W. Thompson, "Relation of Jobbers and Commission Men to the Handling of Produce," Annals of the American Academy of Political and Social Sciences, Vol. L, November, 1913, p. 60.

[36]Converse, Huegy, and Mitchell, op. cit., p. 269.

[37]Foulke, op. cit., p. 188.

[38]Ibid., p. 189.

[39]Ibid., p. 7.

[40]Frank G. Urner, "Wholesale City Distribution of Farm Products," Annals of the American Academy of Political and Social Sciences Vol. L, November, 1913, p. 70.

[41]Ibid., pp. 70-1.

[42]See chart of wholesale prices page 62.

[43]Melvin T. Copeland, The Cotton Manufacturing Industry of the United States (Cambridge: Harvard University Press, 1917), p. 195.

[44]Paul T. Cherington, The Commercial Problems of the Woolen and Worsted Industry (Washington: Textile Foundation, Inc., 1932), p. 84.

[45]Copeland, op. cit., p. 209.

[46]Bulletin of the National Association of Wool Manufacturers, 1895 (Boston, 1895), p. 62.

[47]New York Chamber of Commerce, Thirty-Third Annual Report, 1890 (New York, 1891), Part II, p. 81.

[48]Cole, American Carpet Manufacture, op. cit., p. 199.

[49]Ibid., p. 201.

[50]"Cone Mills: Old King Denim," Fortune, January, 1953, p. 87.

[51]Saladin v. Mitchell, 45 III, 79 cited in Edward J. Hill, The Law of Commission (Chicago, 1879), pp. 7-8.

[52]From an examination of the business directories for 1900 in the leading market centers. Not all these trades were represented by brokers in any one center nor were brokers equally important in every trade or center.

[53]Boston Board of Trade, Twenty-Ninth Annual Report, 1882 (Boston, 1883), p. 58.

[54]Report of the Industrial Commission, 1900, Distribution and Marketing of Farm Products (Washington, 1901), Vol. VI, p. 252.

[55]Loc. cit.

[56]Ibid., p. 173.

[57]M.B. Hammond, The Cotton Industry (New York: American Economic Association, 1897), p. 294.

[58]Ibid., p. 295.

[59]Loc. cit.

[60]A. Urban Shirk, Marketing Through Food Brokers (New York: McGraw-Hill Company, Inc., 1939), p. 24.

[61]National Food Brokers Association, Food Brokers (Washington, 1945), p. 3.

[62]L.D.H. Weld, "Marketing Agencies Between Manufacturers and Jobbers," Quarterly Journal of Economics, August, 1917, p. 586.

[63]Loc. cit.

[64]Loc. cit.

[65]R.A. Smith, "The Ninety-Nine Lives of Charlie Soames," Fortune, January, 1953, pp. 100-3.

[66]Weld, op. cit., p. 582.

CHAPTER VI

PARTICULAR COMPETITIVE PROBLEMS ENCOUNTERED BY THE WHOLESALER

Chapters IV and V dealt with the changes and the probable
reasons for the changes which took place among wholesalers in the
United States between 1860 and 1900. As indicated, this was
generally a prosperous era for the individual wholesaler even though
he was constantly confronted with numerous difficulties. Some of the
principal problems arose out of the competitive climate in which
these middlemen functioned. The purpose of this chapter is to
examine some of the particular competitive problems encountered by
the wholesaler during the period, the manner in which the problems
were met, or evaded, and to attempt to assess the net effect of these
phenomena upon the wholesaler and his position in the marketing
structure.

Major Competitors of the Wholesaler

There were, of course, problems resulting from competition
between wholesalers in the same line but these were by no means the
only ones. More important, perhaps, were problems engendered by the
attempts which were being made to eliminate the middlemen. These
efforts were undertaken by consumers' groups as well as by
manufacturers and retailers.

It is generally recognized that there is a wholesale function to
be performed. However, this is not the same as saying that there are

wholesalers' functions nor does it automatically guarantee the wholesaler a place in the marketing mechanism. In the long run these activities will be carried on by whatever type of distributive reorgan-
ization demonstrates that it can function most efficiently and economically. Therein lie the roots of many of the competitive problems
encountered by wholesaler during the period under consideration.

The wholesaler cannot be regarded as an independent entity in
distribution but must be considered as an integral part of the trade
channel. During this period he was subjected to numerous stresses
and strains arising from the wholesaling activities of manufacturers
and retailers and from various consumer movements intended to eliminate the middleman. These activities became especially significant
after about 1880. As has been shown this was the date roughly
marking the disappearance in many lines of the sellers' market.

This change was a basic general cause of the efforts which were
made by manufacturers and retailers to eliminate the wholesaler.
Since the wholesaler does not create form utility it was difficult
for many to see that he was productive. This failure to perceive
that the wholesaler's productivity lay in the creation of time, place
and possession utilities cast doubt upon his desirability and
provided a stimulus for the movement to eliminate him. Other more
specific reasons will be introduced as the discussion progresses.
The presentation is complicated by the intimate inter-relationships
which exist between topics. Attention will be centered first upon

the various attempts made to eliminate the wholesaler, second, upon
the wholesalers' reactions on these attempts, and finally to an
evaluation of the net effect of these actions.

Efforts to Eliminate the Wholesaler

Manufacturers selling direct. There is ample evidence to show
that there was a definite tendency among manufacturers, particularly
during the latter part of the nineteenth century, to bypass the
wholesaler and sell direct to the retailer and/or the consumer.
There was also a tendency for manufacturing firms to integrate
backwards into the markets for partly manufactured goods and raw
materials which had the effect of eliminating some of the wholesalers
in those areas.[1] The present discussion, however, will be centered
on the most important aspect of this three-pronged invasion of the
mercantile field by manufacturers, that of the finished goods market.

The Industrial Commission concluded in 1900 that for some years
previous to that time changes in business methods had tended to
increase the proportion of goods sold without the intermediary
service of independent merchants. The Commission reported that:

> One thing is made clear by the investigation
> of the commission. The importance of the
> middlemen between producer and retail dealer is
> diminishing, and in some instances retail dealers
> themselves are being displaced by the practice of
> direct selling by manufacturers...At present
> there seems to be a very marked decline in the
> jobbing business and, to a less extent, a decline
> also in the commission business.[2]

That this movement was general there can be no doubt. The advertising manager of a firm producing drug specialties said in 1910 that few manufacturers, particularly of advertised trade-marked goods, distributed exclusively through jobbers.[3] He went on to state that in the drug line, for example:

> There is a growing tendency among manufacturers of advertised specialties to sell the cream of the retail trade direct. The largest and most influential retail druggists buy almost everything 'direct' and in most cases get the manufacturer's very best wholesale discounts. As this policy becomes more and more general, the jobber's field is being restricted more and more to the small dealer...[4]

This movement was noted by a number of writers and numerous instances could be mentioned. For example, Shaw wrote in 1912 that:

> Just as the long period of development from a system of barter economy to the early decades of the factory system showed a continuous tendency for increase in the number of middlemen intervening between the producer and the consumer, so recent years have shown a growing tendency to decrease the number of successive steps in distribution. The tendency is apparent in nearly every industry and has been clearly marked in recent years.[5]

More specifically some of the trades referred to in the preceding quotation in which this tendency was apparent were glass, salt, drugs, meat, cordage, and petroleum products.[6]

In his testimony before the Industrial Commission the President of the Pittsburgh Plate Glass Company reported in 1900 that:

> The Pittsburgh Plate Glass Company was at the mercy of the jobbers, who fixed the prices at which glass was sold, and it was determined by

> the consolidated company to establish its own
> branch house and sell its glass directly to the
> consumer. At the present time it has invested in
> the jobbing branch of its business $4,044,000,
> and has warehouses in New York, Brooklyn, Boston,
> Philadelphia, Chicago, St. Louis, Cincinnati,
> Detroit, Cleveland, Minneapolis, Davenport,
> Columbus, Milwaukee, and Omaha, with branch
> offices for the sale of glass at Rochester,
> Baltimore, and Buffalo.[7]

A further example is furnished by the cordage industry. The National Cordage Company was a combination of several firms set up to coordinate operations and sell the output of those firms.[8] They eliminated the traveling and commission men and the business "was practically all jobbing. They did not have any sales agents whatever."[9] This company failed and out of it grew the Standard Rope and Twine Company. Although this firm did sell through wholesalers the major portion of its output was sold through the Union Selling Company. The latter was a subsidiary established expressly to handle the product of Standard. It had wholesaling branches in all sections of the country, thus eliminating many of the wholesalers in the sale of this product.

Similar activity was taking place in other lines. The National Salt Company by 1900 was selling direct to retailers and doing away with other middlemen. The President of the company stated that this was being accomplished by selling direct "to the retail grocer who passes goods in small quantities to the consumers. We appeal to him by personal solicitation of salesmen and by letters."[10]

It is evident from the above that during the latter part of the period in question the wholesalers' position was being weakened by the efforts of the manufacturers to contact retailers directly. There were a number of reasons for this tendency on the part of the manufacturers.

Increased competition among manufacturers was perhaps the major factor in influencing them to seek out the retailer rather than selling through wholesalers. Previous to the appearance of the buyers' market about 1880 the producer had little difficulty disposing of his output and was willing to let the wholesaler handle his products. Before the completion of the railroad net many manufacturers enjoyed what amounted practically to a local monopoly in the area in which they were located and competition was therefore less severe.

This point is borne out by the evidence collected by the Industrial Commission which concluded that:

> A specially significant feature of the
> increase in production and in means of
> transportation has been the widening of
> markets...Today in many industries the producers
> in widely separated sections of the country, and
> in widely separated countries themselves, compete
> with one another in many markets...In many cases
> the widening of the area of competition has
> increased its intensity. The more or less
> monopolistic control of particular local markets,
> which was formerly enjoyed by many manufacturers,
> has largely disappeared.[11]

A second reason, closely related to the first, was the rapid increase in the average size of manufacturing concerns during this period. When the manufacturer was small he lacked knowledge of the market and was often inadequately financed. The wholesalers supplied market information and financial assistance and so were important to the manufacturer. Speaking of the period Lewis states that, "when manufacturers needed money, they pledged output at a price to their jobber, who eventually owned them."[12]

When the manufacturer became larger he was better able to perform for himself these and other functions which had formerly made the wholesaler indispensable. The proposition that, in many cases, there is an inverse relation between the size of manufacturing firms and the importance of wholesalers to those firms is substantiated by the finding of the Industrial Commission that "The practice of making direct sales to retailers or consumers has been especially common in the case of the great industrial combinations."[13]

Still other reasons for the manufacturer's efforts to sell direct lay in alleged inefficiency and dictatorial conduct on the part of wholesalers. The Pittsburgh Plate Glass Company, for instance, gave as its reason for establishing its own distributing branches the dictatorial conduct of its jobbers who attempted, through their national association, to tell the manufacturers what wholesale merchants they should sell and at what prices the product should be offered.[14]

Since the wholesaler handled many hundreds of items he was unable to give much attention to any one. The manufacturer often became impatient with this neglect of his product by the wholesaler and set up his own organization to see that the goods were sold effectively.

In reply to a series of questions on this subject the sales manager of a manufacturing firm said:

> In response to your third question as to what jobbers are doing to get in wrong with manufacturers and retailers, let me reply that some of them are doing almost everything imaginable, though most of them appear to be acting pretty decently. Personally, I am disposed to think that the jobbers' shortcomings are not born of 'pure cussedness', but rather from shortsighted conceptions on one side and under the lash of strenuous competition on the other.[15]

The use of brand names and trade-marks by manufacturers facilitated direct selling. This made it possible for the manufacturer to identify himself with his product in the minds of consumers and thus gave him a better grip on the market. The use of distributors' brands which had its beginnings during this period provided another motive for the manufacturer in his efforts to bypass the wholesaler. Manufacturers charged that wholesale merchants were continually attempting to substitute their own brands for those of the manufacturers thus limiting the sale of the latter.

Large retailers buying direct. After the Civil War there was a noticeable tendency toward the development of large-scale retailing. This was another factor which tended to weaken the position of the wholesalers, particularly the wholesale merchant. Referring again to the findings of the Industrial Commission it is reported that:

Another powerful influence which has tended
to reduce the importance of the wholesale dealer
has been the great increase in the size of the
retail establishments in many cases. Department
stores buy goods of many classes, often in
exceedingly large quantities, in some cases
purchasing the entire output of mills. Moreover,
many stores dealing in special classes of
articles have so developed that their purchases
are on a scale much larger than before. These
large retailers, therefore, tend more and more to
deal directly with manufacturers, in fact often
ordering in advance of actual production the
particular styles which they desire. This latter
practice relieves the manufacturer of risk,
minimizing the time between the production and
the consumption of goods. The large retail
dealer knows, at least so it is claimed by the
representatives of department stores, more
accurately than the jobber just what the wants of
the consumer are, and the danger of producing
unsalable commodities is therefore reduced by
this change in the methods of business.[16]

In his testimony before the Commission John Wannamaker claimed

that one of the chief economies secured by department stores was

buying directly from the manufacturer thus eliminating the commission

men and jobbers.[17]

Other prominent retail merchants were of similar opinions. One

department store executive speaking in 1900 stated that department

stores had materially decreased the number of middlemen between the

manufacturer and the retailer by buying direct from manufacturers

whenever possible.[18]

Numerous other similar instances and opinions could be cited.

The above, however, are sufficient to support the point that before

1900 there was a tendency among large retailers to bypass the

middlemen and purchase direct from the manufacturer.

Probably somewhat less important in their effects upon the wholesalers, but nevertheless a factor, were similar efforts by groups of smaller retailers to buy direct. The editor of a Chicago retail trade journal described the situation in 1900 as follows:

> We have started a wholesale drug house over here. So many druggists have got together and are buying together now to buy cheaper. There is now a firm or combination in Chicago to follow a combination that is now in existence in the city of Baltimore, where the retailers themselves have a large store, a wholesale house, patronized by 800 retailers. In the city of New York the retailers generally buy their teas, coffees, and cereals together direct from the manufacturers. In the city of Cincinnati they have 500 retailers buying together. We have the same conditions here in this state in some small towns. It is now started here. It is only a short time till the jobber will be something of the past, and I believe now that the consumer ought to get that benefit.[19]

This practice of group buying gradually became more widespread and there were a number of these organizations operating successfully before 1900. In the drug trade, for example, a cooperative group was organized in New York city in 1887 under the name of New York Consolidated Drug Company. The Philadelphia Wholesale Drug Company was organized in 1888 as a buying club and by 1932 had become the largest retailer-owned wholesale drug company in the United States with annual sales between seven and eight million dollars.[20]

A similar group was also established in the grocery trade in Philadelphia during 1888. This was the Frankford Grocery Company which began as a credit and collection agency. The Girard Grocery Company was established in Philadelphia shortly thereafter.[21] The

founding of the Baltimore Wholesale Grocery Company in 1887 is
considered to be the beginning of the cooperative chain movement
although the Paterson Grocers Association was also formed in that
year for the purpose of group buying.[22]

These early cooperative chains were organized so that the
retailers could buy as a group, or buy and merchandise together, in
order that they would be in a position to buy directly from the
manufacturer thus earning for themselves a part of the charges
formerly paid to wholesalers.[23] Other activities were undertaken
later but the effect has been, from the beginning, to weaken the
position of the independent wholesale merchant.

There was also a tendency on the part of individual retailers to
become wholesale merchants. It was pointed out in 1903 that:

> During the last thirty or forty years, large
> jobbing houses have grown up not only in cities
> like Chicago, San Francisco, St. Paul and St.
> Louis, but also in many smaller towns, until we
> now find it to be a frequent ambition of
> retailers to class themselves as jobbers, and
> handle the wholesale business in their own
> neighborhood. This ramification of the jobbing
> business is having its effect on the larger
> jobbers. New York, Philadelphia, Chicago and St.
> Louis no longer have a monopoly of the jobbing
> business, although these large cities are not
> easily deprived of the advantages to which they
> are naturally entitled by their size.[24]

The growth of corporate chains and mail order houses was another
competitive element which was not without its effect upon the
wholesalers before 1900 although the former did not experience their
major development until the twentieth century.

The so-called catalog jobbers aroused some comment in wholesale circles in the late 1890's but apparently did not constitute a serious problem for most wholesalers. It was said that, "This business has had a remarkable expansion, particularly in the West, but side by side has gone the development and increase of the jobbing business."[25] Judging by the amount of opposition and comment in trade papers wholesalers were apparently feeling the effect by this time of the mail-order houses selling direct to consumers.[26]

Such were the activities of retailers during this period which tended to weaken the position of the wholesaler.

Farmers' efforts to eliminate the middlemen. Shortly after the Civil War the Granger movement began. This was the leading farmers' movement which had as its major economic objective the removal of the middleman or, at least, a drastic reduction in his allegedly disproportionate charges. An authoritative source states that:

> ...it was against the exactions of these middlemen that much of the wrath of the farmers was directed. From the standpoint of the farmer the middlemen were of two principal classes: the commission merchants and produce buyers through whom he disposed of his products, and the numerous agents and retail dealers through whom he purchased his supplies.[27]

Feeling was high on this point and much of the literature characterized the middlemen as profiteers out to exploit the farmer. It was charged that the middlemen were growing rich at the expense of the farmer who could not progress for this reason.[28]

As farmers the Grangers objected to excessive charges made by the wholesale middlemen through whom they marketed their products. As consumers they felt the prices they paid for goods were unnecessarily inflated by an excessive number of wholesale and retail dealers. These problems they proposed to remedy by cooperative effort. Just what the net effect of this was upon the wholesalers is impossible to say although Buck concludes that a great deal of good resulted from the farmers' attempts at business cooperation.[29] The Industrial Commission concluded that, "It is doubtful whether the Granger of 30 years ago recognizes how fully the ambitions and aims of that organization have been realized in bringing the producer and the consumer nearer together."[30]

This movement also provided a stimulus to the mail-order houses mentioned above. Montgomery Ward, for example, was established in 1872 and took advantage of the situation to advertise that goods could be bought by mail at lower prices because of the elimination of the middleman's profit.

Competitive Efforts and Tools Employed by the Wholesaler

The activities of manufacturers, retailers and consumers discussed above had the effect of weakening the position of the wholesaler and in some cases they probably eliminated him. In addition, there was considerable competition among wholesalers in the same line. As a result of these things the wholesaler found himself confronted with serious problems. The present section will be concerned with an examination of some of the steps taken by wholesalers, particularly wholesale merchants, in meeting these problems.

Formation of associations. Increasing competition led wholesale merchants in many lines to form themselves into associations in order to protect and further their interests by concerted action. This trend toward the formation of associations may be said really to have begun with the founding of the Western Wholesale Drug Association in 1876. This was followed by the establishment of similar organizations in various parts of the country in other trades.

There were numerous local or regional associations formed in hardware and in other lines after this time. The National Hardware Association formed in 1895 was an outgrowth of one of these.[31] In 1862 the eastern druggists joined with those of the west to set up the National Wholesale Druggists' Association.[32] In 1888 the Wholesale Grocers' Association of New York City came into existence.[33]

There was, during these years then, a clear tendency among wholesale merchants to establish trade associations. The major incentives were to avoid competitive abuses and excesses among the members of the particular trade and to secure a unified force with which to face other competitive problems. With feeling high among consumers and with manufacturers and retailers taking positive steps to bypass the wholesaler the latter purpose was equal in importance

with the first. It is interesting to note that it was not until
after 1880 that the majority of these associations were formed. This
is the date which marks roughly the disappearance of the sellers'
market.

The individual associations carried on numerous activities
designed to meet the particular problems encountered during this
period. The purposes of the Western Wholesale Drug Association are
set forth in the preamble to its constitution:

> In order to create a permanent social
> feeling between the wholesale druggists of the
> West (United States)--to obliterate the feeling
> of distrust and jealousy that seems to exist--to
> correct excessive and unmercantile competition--
> to remove by concert of action, all evils and
> customs that are against good policy and sound
> business principles--to establish rules and
> regulations that all differences and grievances
> may be fairly and equitably adjusted--for this
> purpose we, the undersigned, form ourselves into
> an association, to be known as the Western
> Wholesale Drug Association (National Wholesale
> Druggists' Association).34

The associations generally were credited with benefiting the
members and the trade simply by bringing competitors into close
social contact and destroying personal animosities which had often
led to competitive excesses.[35]

The following quotation shows the importance attained by
wholesalers' associations by 1900 and indicates another of their
general activities which were advantageous to members:

> These associations also stand in important
> relation to the manufacturers, and have
> frequently been able to induce them to adopt
> better methods in the disposal of their goods.

> The associations have taken the view that jobbers
> are the natural outlet for the manufacturer, who
> should regard the jobber as his selling agent,
> and not his enemy, and that their interests are
> joint and often identical. Manufacturers have in
> many cases readily responded to this liberal
> idea, and an element of harmony has thus been
> brought into their relations. In all such
> matters, jobbing associations have been highly
> useful, while in these days of mammoth
> corporations and trusts, they have often been
> able to command a hearing where the individual
> jobber would have been ignored.[36]

Other problems were handled through the associations which could

not have been met so successfully otherwise. For example, the

National Wholesale Druggists' Association was active in the movement

toward shorter credit terms. Their recommendations were generally

some years in advance of actual practice, but, nevertheless, were

undoubtedly influential.[37] Many of these organizations have grown

and developed and handle a wide range of management and merchandising

problems.

Many of the associations were actively attempting to reverse the

tendency of manufacturers to sell direct to retailers. Their actions

on this problem generally took the form of resolutions condemning the

practice but were apparently rather ineffectual.

As a matter of fact, some of the associations became so

aggressive in their relations with manufacturers that their efforts

led to charges of dictatorial conduct and resulted in actions by

manufacturers which were directly opposite of what the associations

had hoped to accomplish. This was the case, for example, in the

glass industry.

The Chairman of the Commercial Department of the Pittsburgh Plate Glass Company gave as one of that company's reasons for establishing its own wholesaling organization the undue pressure which had been exerted upon it by its wholesale dealers.[38] He charged that the combination of wholesalers in the glass trade had become so powerful as to be able to dictate prices at which glass would be sold to consumers and the prices which manufacturers should receive. By doing its own wholesaling the Pittsburgh Plate Glass Company was able to do away with this.

The net effect of the wholesale associations, however, was to greatly benefit the individual member in his efforts to improve his business methods and to cope with competitive problems which arose during this period.

Private brands. The practice of wholesale merchants of placing their own brands on certain items was discussed earlier.[39] It should, of course, be borne in mind that this was a competitive tool. For one thing the wholesale merchant established his own brand in order to build a reputation for the firm and get a better grip on the market. His own brand could not be taken from him as could the manufacturers' brands.

To some extent, however, there was a circular relationship between manufacturers' and wholesalers' brands which in some cases proved disadvantageous to the wholesale merchant. As the use of manufacturers' brands spread the merchant felt his position being assailed and weakened so he turned to the use of private brands. This in turn brought from the manufacturers renewed charges of alleged unfair business practices such as substitution,[40] that is, substituting a private brand when a manufacturers' brand had been ordered by the retailer.

This practice, perhaps, was not so frequent after 1900 as before. However, when asked if he had encountered this problem the manager of a firm producing and advertising grocery specialties reported in 1910 that he had:

> ...I call it nothing less than stealing. Many jobbers won't act like this, you must understand but there are enough of them that will, so that our selling channels are often seriously blocked up. A jobber that has private brands to sell in competition with those of houses that advertise must walk a very straight line to avoid falling under the suspicion of the manufacturer. Some jobbers hate protected prices. Dickering and trade deals and secret bargains have been the rule so long in former days that jobbing houses which are in a rut cannot understand the spirit of the new era. Some of them will go shameful lengths to undermine the sales of a widely advertised brand. But manufacturers like Procter and Gamble, the Shredded Wheat Biscuit Company, Kellog's Toasted Corn Flake Company and the Cream of Wheat Company, who have got their fighting spirit up, are making things unpleasant for those jobbers who are putting sand into the gear-box.[41]

This practice of substitution simply gave the manufacturer another incentive to attempt to bypass the jobber wherever possible and, in any case, to advertise as much as was feasible in the hope that the jobber would be forced to handle his product. Manufacturers' associations were set up, in some instances,

specifically to deal with this problem. It was proposed by some
manufacturers that the so-called "manufacturing jobber" be allowed a
smaller margin than others on the manufacturers' brands. There is no
evidence to indicate, however, that this proposal was ever made
effective.

In spite of all the charges and counter-measures by manufacturers
it appears that, on balance, the wholesale merchant probably
benefited from the use of distributors' brands as a competitive tool.

Factor or rebate plan. After the Civil War there ensued a
period of considerable economic expansion followed by depression
beginning in 1873. Then came the appearance in many trades of the
buyers' market which served to intensify competition which already
existed among wholesalers within particular lines. One of the
principal manifestations of these charges was severe price-
competition among the wholesale merchants.

That this problem was a serious one is indicated by the remarks
of the President of the Western Wholesale Drug Association in 1879:

> Is it right and just upon an even market to
> offer and sell even a few articles at a price
> less than, or so near to, the purchase price as
> to fail to pay their proportionate part of the
> actual expense of doing business? If such a
> course be pursued for the purpose of enticing
> away or dissatisfying the customers of others, or
> for the purpose of making what are called
> 'leaders' in trade, by attempting to impress
> purchasers with the idea that the merchant is
> offering all his goods at an equally close
> margin, it is an evil that should be removed...
> This style of doing business is prolific of
> evils, and when once adopted, or suffered to
> creep in, is liable to increase its proportions

> and multiply 'leaders' and other evils to an
> alarming extent. It also invites the handling of
> inferior and adulterated goods, and other nefari-
> ous practices which we cannot too strongly condemn.[42]

In a number of trades the net result of these actions was that it became impossible to make a profit on many of the goods which the wholesale merchant handled. As a remedy many of these middlemen turned to the rebate plan and worked, both as individuals and through their associations, for its widespread adoption.

In essence the rebate plan was a simple one and, although it varied in detail as between different trades, the principle was essentially the same in all cases. Briefly, the plan called for the manufacturer to sell his goods to wholesalers at a given price, at the same time establishing the price at which the goods were to be resold to retailers. If after a predetermined time the wholesaler had not cut the resale price he received a rebate from the manufacturer on the goods sold and this constituted his profit.[43]

This plan was used in a number of instances and appears to have worked with some degree of success, at least for a while. The origin of the rebate idea is rather obscure but one of the first groups to adopt it was the wholesale drug trade in 1876.[44] In discussing the founding of the druggists' association and the subsequent workings of its various committees John McKesson pointed out in 1895 that:

> ...the committee on rebates has really
> effected the most important changes in trade
> matters. Up to that time there had not been more
> than a dozen large distributing centers in the
> United States; now, by the working of the rebate

> system, almost all towns of 50,000 inhabitants
> have one or more wholesale druggists, who are
> placed on an equal footing with the largest
> buyer, and each one supplies the retailers in his
> neighborhood.[45]

There were, of course, other factors in the phenomenon which McKesson describes. Nevertheless, his remarks were typical of the generally favorable attitude among wholesalers concerning the rebate plans.

The use of rebates was particularly common among the industrial combinations formed during the 1890's. There were charges from some quarters that this system was simply a means by which the combinations could maintain a monopolistic control over the wholesale merchants. This charge was not true, however, for it was usually at the suggestion of the wholesale merchants that the manufacturers adopted the plans. In the case of the sugar combination, testimony showed that:

> Competition among the wholesalers had
> resulted in depriving them of any profits
> whatever, and had even, in many cases, forced
> them to sell at a loss. In order to avoid this
> difficulty the wholesalers themselves petitioned
> the American Sugar Refining Company to adopt the
> factor plan, and after a consideration of the
> matter, as an accommodation to the wholesaler,
> the plan was adopted.[46]

These plans were tried with some success in the sale of such items as sugar, drugs, whisky, baking powder and soap.[47] The evidence indicates that from the point of view of the wholesalers concerned the rebates helped to reduce some of the ills resulting from the intense competition during this time and provided those distributors with a profit which otherwise could not have been earned.

Summary

Changing status of the wholesaler. By way of summarization of
the foregoing discussion it is worthwhile to note the effect that
these phenomena had in changing the status of the wholesaler as a
figure in the trade channel.

The evidence shows conclusively that there was a tendency among
manufacturers, particularly during the latter part of the period
under consideration, to bypass the wholesaler and sell direct to
retailers and/or consumers. Competitive pressures largely account
for this movement although, as indicated, there were other factors.

Similarly, there was a noticeable, trend among retailers to buy
direct wherever possible in an effort to buy cheaper and to secure
the wholesale margins for themselves. There were also movements
among farmers designed to eliminate some of the wholesale middlemen.
In addition, competition among wholesalers in a given line became
severe. All this created serious problems for the wholesaler and
tended to weaken his position.

Meanwhile the wholesalers were not standing idly by. Wholesale
merchants were forming themselves into associations for concerted
action. Many became more specialized in order to provide better
service to retailers who were tending toward specialization. The
rebate plan was recommended by wholesale merchants to reduce
price-competition and put themselves in a better position. Some
wholesale merchants introduced their own brands not only because they

saw possibilities of larger margins but also to counteract the manufacturer's tendency to sell his own goods direct.

The result of these counteractivities on the part of the wholesale middlemen was undoubtedly to help strengthen their position. Nevertheless, the consensus among manufacturers, wholesalers, retailers and others at this time apparently was that the wholesaler was declining in importance, the merchant more than the agent wholesaler.

In spite of these opinions it is doubtful if, in general, wholesalers were declining. It is more probable that as a group they were continuing to increase in importance and were handling ever greater quantities of goods but that by the end of the nineteenth century the rate of growth was decelerating.

This conclusion is not inconsistent with the evidence presented for many of the wholesalers who were most vociferous in complaining about the decline were the leading ones located in the larger centers. They were feeling the effects of increased competition resulting from the establishment of new local jobbing points in the smaller towns and cities and so generalized falsely from their own experience that wholesalers were on the brink of annihilation.

On the other hand, it has been shown in the preceding chapters that this was generally a prosperous period for wholesalers and instances of their growth have been cited. This would tend to support the above conclusion.

It is clear, moreover, that there was a considerable change in the status of wholesale middlemen during the latter part of the century, particularly among the wholesale merchants. In 1860 the wholesale merchant was becoming the dominant factor in the trade channel, manufacturer-wholesale merchant-retailer-consumer, but by 1900 he was on the defensive and was having difficulty in justifying his position. Nevertheless, wholesalers were handling large quantities of goods and were an important cog in the distributive mechanism.

FOOTNOTES - CHAPTER VI

[1]Edward D. Jones, "The Manufacturer and the Domestic Market," Annals of the American Academy of Political and Social Science, January, 1905, p. 1.

[2]Final Report of the Industrial Commission (Washington: Government Printing Office, 1902), Vol. XIX, p. 546.

[3]Printers' Ink, August 25, 1910, p. 38.

[4]Loc. cit.

[5]A.W. Shaw, "Some Problems in Market Distribution," Quarterly Journal of Economics, August, 1912, p. 728.

[6]Edward D. Jones, op. cit., p. 8.

[7]Testimony of Mr. John Pitcairn, President, Pittsburgh Plate Glass Company, Report of the Industrial Commission, Trusts and Industrial Combinations (Washington: Government Printing Office, 1901), Vol. XIII, p. 227.

[8]Report of the Industrial Commission, Vol. XIII, p. 127.

[9]Ibid., p. 159.

[10]Ibid., p. 266.

[11]Ibid., p. 545.

[12]E.S. Lewis, Ed., The Credit Man and His Work (Detroit: Bookkeeper Publishing Company, 1904), p. 32.

[13]Final Report of the Industrial Commission, op. cit., p. 546.

[14]Loc. cit.

[15]Printers' Ink, September 22, 1910, p. 32.

[16]Final Report of the Industrial Commission, op. cit., p. 547.

[17]Report of the Industrial Commission, Labor, Manufactures and General Business (Washington: Government Printing Office, 1901), p. 455.

[18]Testimony of S.W. Woodward before the Industrial Commission, op. cit., p. 736.

[19]Testimony of S.W. Roth before the Industrial Commission, op. cit., p. 711.

[20]National Wholesale Conference, Report of Committee II, Economic Factors Affecting Wholesaling (Washington: Chamber of Commerce of the United States, 1929), p. 17; U.S.--Federal Trade Commission, Chain Stores: Cooperative Drug and Hardware Stores (Washington: Government Printing Office, 1932), p. 7.

[21]National Wholesale Conference, op. cit., p. 17.

[22]P.D. Converse, H.W. Huegy, and R.V. Mitchell, The Elements of of Marketing (New York: Prentice-Hall, Inc., 1952), p. 418; Federal Trade Commission, Chain Stores; Cooperative Grocery Chains, op. cit., p. 10.

[23]Senate Documents, 72nd Congress, 1st Session, Chain Stores (Washington: Government Printing Office, 1932), p. XVI.

[24]J.H. Ritter, "Present Day Jobbing," Annals of the American Academy of Political and Social Science, December, 1903, p. 40.

[25]Ibid., p. 43.

[26]See, for example, Iron Age, January 4, 1906, pp. 147, 152, 159-60, 165.

[27]S.J. Buck, The Granger Movement (Cambridge: Harvard University Press, 1913), p. 16.

[28]E.W. Martin, History of the Grange Movement (Philadelphia: National Publishing Company, 1873), p. 297.

[29]Buck, op. cit., p. 278.

[30]Report of the Industrial Commission, Distribution of Farm Products (Washington: Government Printing Office, 1901), p. 6.

[31]T.J. Fernley, "The National Hardware Association," Iron Age, January 4, 1906, p. 157.

[32]A History of the National Wholesale Druggists' Association (New York: The Association, 1924), p. 11.

[33]Testimony of G.W. Smith, President, Wholesale Grocers' Association, in Industrial Commission, Report on Trust and Industrial Combinations (Washington: Government Printing Office, 1900), Vol. I, p. 55.

[34]History of the National Wholesale Druggists' Association, op. cit., p. 19.

[35]Ibid., pp. 85-6; Ritter, op. cit., p. 45; T.J. Fernley, op. cit., p. 158.

[36]Ritter, op. cit., pp. 45-6.

[37]See page 147.

[38]Testimony of Mr. W.W. Heroy, before the Industrial Commission, Trusts and Industrial Combinations, Vol. XIII, op. cit., p. 244.

[39]See page 132.

[40]R.W. Gage, "The Mix-Up Centering Around the Jobber," Printers' Ink, August 18, 1910, p. 11.

[41]Loc. cit.

[42]History of the National Wholesale Druggists' Association, op. cit., pp. 29-30.

[43]Industrial Commission, Trust and Industrial Combinations, Vol. I, p. 21; C.W. Depew, One Hundred Years of American Commerce (New York: D.O. Haynes and Co., 1895), p. 612.

[44]History of the National Wholesale Druggists' Association, op. cit., p. 30.

[45]Depew, op. cit., p. 612.

[46]Industrial Commission, Trust and Industrial Combinations, Vol. I, pp. 21, 64; see also, in section three, the testimony of G.W. Smith, President, Wholesale Grocers' Association of New York City, pp. 55-68.

[47]Ibid., pp. 59, 61; Ritter, op. cit., p. 16; New York Price Current, March 13, 1897.

CHAPTER VII

SUMMARY AND CONCLUSIONS

The changes which took place in the wholesale structure of the
United States between 1860 and 1900 cannot be attributed to any one
specific cause. To enumerate all the influences which had a bearing
upon these developments would require a detailed description of the
pattern of economic growth of the country. Nevertheless, a number of
particular cause and effect relationships are discernible in the
evolution of the wholesaler and his markets during the last four
decades of the nineteenth century.

Notable among the major developments of this period was the
rapid increase in the size of the markets. Among other things the
size of markets depends upon the number of people, quantity of
purchasing power and willingness to buy. In 1900 the population of
the United States was more than twice as large as in 1860 while per
capita national income also doubled. It was inevitable that this
phenomenon should have far-reaching implications for the wholesaler
and the centers from which wholesale trade was controlled.

In 1860 there were eight major wholesale centers which dominated
the flow of internal trade. Of these New York was most prominent;
its preeminence was founded upon superior port and transportation
facilities. The latter tapped rich interior areas which provided
goods for export and, more important, furnished a broad market for

imports. New York maintained its leadership in the ensuing decades by virtue of its geographic advantages, the extension of its superiority in water transportation facilities into the railroad era, and its position as the principal financial center of the country.

Also growing in absolute terms, but declining relatively, were the other major coastal centers Philadelphia, Boston and Baltimore. Philadelphia and Boston competed with New York for the western and southern trade as well as that of New England. Baltimore and Philadelphia were competitors for the trade of the interior and the South. At the same time, in the South New Orleans was declining in relative importance. The development of the Erie Canal and Great Lakes waterways, the rapid expansion of the railroad net, and the early lack of good railroad facilities largely account for the inroads of competing centers on New Orleans' trade area.

While in 1860 most of the wholesale trade of the interior was carried on by Cincinnati, Chicago and St. Louis this situation had changed considerably by 1900. By that time jobbing points had been established in other interior cities as well as in numerous smaller towns. This development was, in part, a result of such broad economic phenomena as the continual westward movement of population, extension of the railroad system, and improvements in communication facilities. In addition, some of the older established centers, particularly those in the East, were losing trade to the newer western centers. This was especially noticeable after economic disturbances such as the Panic of 1873, for instance, when buying tended to be done in smaller quantities, credits were shortened and retailers were anxious to buy closer to home.

Chicago strengthened its dominant position as the leading center of trade in the interior largely on the basis of advantages in railroad transportation and location. In the meantime, although continuing to grow absolutely, other cities developed less rapidly and some, such as Cincinnati, declined in relative importance as wholesale centers.

The pattern of growth was similar for most of the centers. The major developments took place first in the cities whose location afforded the greatest advantage in transportation relative to sources of supply and markets. Thus, the seaboard centers were the first to gain preeminence in wholesaling followed closely by the interior cities located on inland waterways such as Cincinnati, Chicago, and St. Louis. Then, with the development of the railroads, jobbing points were established in smaller cities and towns which were not located on major waterways.

By 1900 these local wholesalers were becoming increasingly important and were making inroads on the business of wholesalers located in the larger centers. This new local competition helps to account, in part at least, for the statements by some of the leading businessmen that wholesalers were declining. Actually the census data show an increase in the number of persons engaged as wholesale merchants and dealers from 31,086 in 1890 to 42,326 in 1900. The establishment of local wholesale firms probably accounts for the larger part of this gain.

Throughout the period there were a number of different types of wholesale middlemen operating in these markets. Among them were the wholesale merchants, shipping merchants, importers and exporters, auctioneers, commission merchants, brokers and manufacturers' agents.

During the period 1860 to 1900 the wholesale merchant was one of the more important middlemen in the internal trade of the United States. He performed a vital service in bringing together the products of a large number of small producers and selling them to a large number of small retailers on credit and in small quantities. During this period the wholesale merchant performed practically all the functions with which he is commonly associated today.

One of the more important changes made in the wholesale merchants' operations during this time was the tendency toward specialization. In 1860 semi-jobbers were probably more numerous than merchants selling at wholesale only but, by 1900, the larger and more important wholesale firms were selling at wholesale only and fewer were combining agent and merchant function. In addition to this functional specialization there was also a trend toward product specialization.

The rapid expansion of the markets was the principal facilitating factor behind this trend. As the firm's volume of sales increased it became more profitable, in many cases, to sell a narrower line at wholesale only. Another important influence was the tendency toward specialization among the retailers whom the wholesale merchants served.

Aggressive selling and sales promotion by wholesale merchants was practicallly unknown before the Civil War. In the ensuing four decades these wholesalers began to make wide use of such selling tools as traveling salesmen, advertising, illustrated catalogs, distributors' brands, special deals and similar promotional devices. This was largely a manifestation of the shift from a sellers to a buyers' market by about 1880. As competition became more intense the wholesale merchant increased his selling efforts. By 1875 salesmen were calling on the trade at practically every place of any importance in the country and the practice of retailers of making regular buying trips to the central market was no longer customary. The use of illustrated catalogs really began about 1880. By 1900, although they were to become more widespread later, there were a number of well-known wholesalers' brands.

Thus, although the economic environment in the 1860's and early 70's was such that the wholesaler had little difficulty in selling his goods, this situation changed and the wholesale merchant was continually attempting to adjust to the new conditions. Even though the quantitative data are not complete they, along with the other evidence presented, seems to indicate that these efforts were attended by some degree of success.

Following the Civil War the shipping merchants declined in importance. These middlemen were wholesale merchants engaged primarily in foreign trade. With increases in domestic production and the widening of home markets, foreign trade, and its institutions, tended to decline in relative importance. The shipping merchants did not specialize by commodities and they carried on both a transportation and merchandising operation. Firms specializing by commodities and functions could operate more efficiently and as they increased in importance the shipping merchant declined. Among the former were importing, commission, banking and transportation specialists.

The increasing size of American business firms and improvements in transportation and communication links with foreign suppliers and markets facilitated direct contact without the services of the shipping merchant. Changing conditions gradually reduced the necessity for the shipping merchants' services and, in the long run, no middleman can survive unless he performs an essential function economically.

Importers continued the tendency to specialize by commodities after the Civil War but their position was being weakened by increasing participation of other types of organizations in the importing business, by high tariffs, and by increasing competition

from domestic goods. Among manufacturers there was a growing
tendency to import goods themselves.

The rapid expansion of the markets during this period accounted
largely for the importance of agent wholesalers. The more
specialized appear to have increased in importance while the less
specialized declined relatively. These agents were handling
considerable quantities of farm products and the manufacturers found
them an economical means of reaching distant or scattered markets.

After the Civil War auctions declined in importance as a method
of sale at wholesale. Auctions had handled large quantities of
foreign goods and as these decreased in relative importance so did
the auctions. Furthermore, there were other types of agent
wholesalers who made serious inroads on the auctioners' business.
Selling agents became important in the sale of textiles of which
large quantities had been sold at auction. Brokers also provided
serious competition and some of the auctioneers charged that they
were responsible for the decline of auction sales. With the
increased use of traveling salesmen it was easier and cheaper for
country merchants to buy at home than to travel to the central
markets to attend auctions.

Throughout this time commission merchants were important in the
sale of many products but, like the auctioneers, they appear to have
been decreasing in relative importance. These merchants did not
specialize as much as did some of the other agent middlemen and it
was not uncommon to find them performing several types of agent

functions or combining agent and merchant operations. The commission merchant could not, in many cases, offer as efficient service as some of the more specialized middlemen.

Selling agents were particularly important in the sale of textiles. They performed two important functions for their principals, those of selling and financing. Following the Civil War there was an effort on the part of larger manufacturers to eliminate the selling agent but he continued as an important outlet for the product of smaller mills through 1900, especially those in the South. As the manufacturers became larger, better acquainted with the markets and financially stronger the selling agent became less essential to him.

It was not unusual to find a selling agent purchasing the mills he represented. In some cases this was probably because the mills had become inextricably involved financially and, in others, because the agent wanted to insure his position. There were also some mills which, under the pressure of competition, absorbed the selling houses in an effort to lower costs.

Some manufacturers abandoned the use of selling agents in favor of direct sale or sale through brokers. The latter were an integral part of the distribution machinery in 1860 and continued thereafter to increase in importance. By 1900 merchandise brokers were common in the marketing channels of a wide range of products. There was considerably more specialization among brokers than among commission merchants. This would seem to account, in part at least, for the former's efficiency. The investigations of the Industrial Commission showed that brokers were operating economically in many lines. One of the reasons for the declining importance of the commission merchant in cotton, for example, was the increasing amount of interior buying being done through brokers.

Manufacturers' agents were less important during this period although they were developing rapidly by 1900. These agents combined the output of a number of producers which meant they could handle the products of any one with relative economy. They were most important to manufacturers who did not need financial assistance but who desired to sell part of their output, perhaps in new or distant markets, through agents.

In general, this was a period of prosperity and growth for most wholesalers; yet it was not without its problems. Some of the more important of these arose from the attempts of manufacturers, retailers and consumers to eliminate the middlemen. This movement assumed various forms but it is clear that there was an effort on the part of retailers and manufacturers to buy and sell without the services of the wholesalers. Meanwhile, the wholesalers, particularly the wholesale merchants, were attempting to improve their position by the use of such countermeasures as increased advertising and selling effort, the use of wholesalers' brands and formation of associations for group action.

Since no quantitative aggregate data are available it is not possible to assess accurately the net effect of these activities upon the wholesalers' position. The comments, testimony, and writings of manufacturers, retailers, wholesalers and others in the last decade of the nineteenth century, however, generally agree that the wholesalers were declining in importance at that time; the merchant more than the agent wholesalers.

Opinions do not make facts, of course, and a safer conclusion would seem to be that the competitive environment and efforts to eliminate the middlemen probably served to decelerate the rate of growth of the wholesalers but, with one or two exceptions, they continued to develop, at least absolutely. There is little doubt, however, that the qualitative position of the wholesaler, especially the wholesale merchant, was altered between 1860 and 1900. In the earlier part of the period the wholesaler had, in many cases, been the dominant figure but by 1900 he was on the defensive.

In short, it is clear that vast changes took place among wholesalers during the period under consideration and that the nature and scope of their operations in 1900 differed considerably from what they had been in 1860.

Notable among these changes by 1900 were the following:

1. In absolute terms, at least, wholesalers were handling far greater quantities of goods than they had in 1860. This is indicated by the data in Table II, page 12.

2. In 1860 the wholesale trade of the country was largely controlled from the leading wholesale centers discussed in Chapter II. By 1900, however, numerous jobbing points were being established in smaller towns and cities and, in many lines, were challenging the dominance of the leading centers.

3. Throughout the period there was a clearly discernible tendency toward specialization. By 1900 wholesale firms which carried on a general operation had been or were being replaced by firms which were more highly specialized both in terms of products and functions.

4. In contrast to 1860, wholesalers in 1900 were attempting to sell more aggressively. Their principal sales weapons were traveling salesmen, catalogs and a limited amount of advertising of various types.

5. Partly as an effort to strengthen their position wholesale merchants introduced their own brands during this period. No instances of the use of wholesalers' brands in 1860 could be found but by 1900 there were a number of well-known ones.

6. By 1900 the position of the wholesale merchant was being weakened as a result of the efforts of manufacturers and retailers to perform the wholesaling functions themselves. The channel of manufacturer-wholesale merchant-retailer-consumer was common but the wholesale merchant was being forced to relinquish his position of dominance and assume a subordinate role in this channel.

It seems reasonable to conclude that the developments which took place among these wholesalers were made primarily in response to changes in basic economic conditions. Those who failed to make the necessary adjustments tended to disappear for, in the long run, no wholesale middleman can survive if he is out of harmony with the economic environment or is not performing an essential function economically. Among the principal economic influences affecting the wholesalers' operations were changes in the size and nature of markets, extension and improvement of transportation facilities, improved communications and increases in the number and size of manufacturing and retailing establishments, all of which was closely tied in with the increases in population, production and income.

BIBLIOGRAPHY

Books and Pamphlets

Abbott, W.L. Competition and Combination in the Wholesale Grocery
    Trade in Philadelphia. Menasha, Wisconsin: Collegiate Press,
    1920.

Albion, R.G. The Rise of the New York Port. New York: Scribners'
    and Sons, 1939.

Andreas, A.T. History of Chicago. Chicago: A.T. Andreas Co., 1886.

Baker, G.W. A Review of the Relative Commercial Progress of New York
    and Philadelphia. Philadelphia: Jackson, 1859.

Baldwin, William H. Traveling Salesmen. Boston, 1874.

Beckman, T.N., and Engle, N.H. Wholesaling. New York: The Ronald
    Press, 1949.

Belcher, W.W. The Economic Rivalry Between St. Louis and Chicago
    1850–1880. New York: Columbia University Press, 1947.

Bisbee, L.H., and Simonds, J.C. Law of the Produce Exchange.
    Chicago: Callaghan and Company, 1884.

Bishop, J.L. A History of American Manufactures. Philadelphia:
    1866, Vol. II.

Bogart, E.L. and Kemmerer, D.S. Economic History of the American
    People. New York: Longmanns, Green, and Company, 1949.

Bogart, E.L., and Thomson, C.M. Readings in Economic History of the
    United States. New York: Longmanns, Green, and Company, 1916.

Bolles, A.S. Industrial History of the United States. Norwich:
    Henry Bill Company, 1881.

Borsodi, Ralph. The Distribution Age. New York: D. Appleton
    Company, 1927.

Briggs, E.P. Fifty Years on the Road. Phildelphia, 1911.

Bruce, W.O. History of Milwaukee. Chicago: S.J. Clarke Publishing
    Company, 1922.

Buck, N.S. The Development of the Organization of Anglo-American
    Trade, 1800-1850. New Haven: Yale University Press, 1925.

Buck, S.J. The Granger Movement. Cambridge: Harvard University
    Press, 1913.

Casseday, Ben. The History of Louisville. Louisville: Hull and
    Brother, 1852.

Cherington, Paul T. Advertising as a Business Force. Associated
    Advertising Clubs of America, 1913.

Cherington, Paul T. The Wool Industry. Chicago: A.W. Shaw Company,
    1916.

Chinn, William Y. The Mercantile Agencies Against Commerce.
    Chicago: Charles H. Kerr & Co., 1896.

Cist, Charles. Sketches and Statistics of Cincinnati in 1859.
    Cincinnati, 1859.

Clark, Victor S. History of Manufactures in the United States, 1860-
    1914. Washington: Carnegie Institute, 1928.

Cole, A.H. Wholesale Commodity Prices in the United States, 1700-
    1861. Cambridge: Harvard University Press, 1938.

Cole, A.H. The American Wool Manufacture. Cambridge: Harvard
    University Press, 1926. 2 vols.

Cole, Arthur H., and Williamson, Harold J. The American Carpet
    Manufacture. Cambridge: Harvard University Press, 1941.

Coman, K. The Industrial History of the United States. New York:
    MacMillan and Company, 1905.

Commercial and Architectural Chicago. Chicago: G.W. Orear, 1887.

Converse, Paul D. Marketing Methods and Policies. New York:
    Prentice-Hall, Inc., 1921.

Copeland, Melvin T. The Cotton Manufacturing Industry of the United
    States. Cambridge: Harvard University Press, 1917.

Curry, J.S. Manufacturing and Wholesale Industries of Chicago.
    Chicago: Thomas B. Poole and Company, 1918.

Dacus, J.A., and Buell, J.W. A Tour of St. Louis or, the Inside Life of a Great City. St. Louis: Western Publishing Co., 1878.

Day, Olive. A History of Commerce. New York: Longmanns, Green and Company, 1914.

Depew, C.M., Ed. One Hundred Years of American Commerce. New York: D.O. Haynes and Co., 1895. 2 vols.

De Voe, T.F. The Market Book. New York, 1862. 2 vols.

Ditchett, S.H. Marshall Field and Company: the Life Story of a Great Concern. New York: Dry Goods Economist, 1922.

Earling, P.R. Whom to Trust: A Practical Treatise on Mercantile Credit. Chicago: Rand, McNally and Company, 1890.

Erdman, H.E. American Produce Markets. Boston: D.C. Heath and Company, 1928.

Ferguson, E.A. Founding of the Cincinnati Southern Railway. Cincinnati: Robert Clarke Company, 1905.

Forbes, B.C. Men Who Are Making America. New York: B.C. Forbes Publishing Company, 1926.

Forbes, Robert B. Personal Reminiscences. Boston: Little, Brown, 1882.

Foulke, R.A. Peaks and Valleys in Wholesale Prices and Business Failures. New York: Dun and Bradstreet, Inc., 1950.

Foulke, R.A. The Sinews of American Commerce. New York: Dun and Bradstreet, 1941.

Frederick, John H. The Development of American Commerce. New York: D. Appleton and Company, 1932.

Freedley, E.T. Philadelphia and Its Manufactures. Philadelphia: Edward Young, 1859.

Goddard, Frederick B. Giving and Getting Credit. New York: F. Tennyson Neely, 1896.

Gowen, F.B. The Railway Problem. Philadelphia: Jackson Brothers, 1881.

Gras, N.S.B. Business and Capitalism: An Introduction to Business History. New York: Crofts, 1939.

Gras, N.S.B. An Introduction to Economic History. New York: Harper and Brothers, 1922.

Gras, N.S.B. and Larson, H. Casebook in American Business History. New York: F.S. Crofts and Company, 1939.

The Great Industries of the United States. Hartford: J.B. Barr and Hyde, 1873.

Hammond, M.B. The Cotton Industry. New York: The Macmillan Company, 1897.

Hazard, W.P. Annals of Philadelphia and Pennsylvania. Philadelphia: E.S. Stuart, 1879. 3 vols.

Hill, Edward J. The Law of Commission. Chicago: 1879.

A History of the National Wholesale Druggists Association. New York: The Association, 1924.

Hollander, J.H. The Cincinnati Southern Railway. Baltimore: The Johns Hopkins Press, 1894.

Hotchkiss, George B. Milestones of Marketing. New York: The Macmillan Company, 1938.

Hillyer, W.H. James Talcott, Merchant. New York: Charles Scribners and Sons, 1937.

Hunt, Freeman. Lives of American Merchants. New York: Derby and Jackson Company, 1858.

Joblin, M. and Company. Cincinnati Past and Present. Cincinnati, 1872.

Johnson, E.H. et. al. History of Domestic and Foreign Commerce of the United States. Washington: Carnegie Institute, 1915. 2 vols.

Jones, Fred M. "The Development of Marketing Channels in the United States to 1920," (Unpublished Manuscript, College of Commerce, University of Illinois, Urbana).

Keeler, V.D. The Commercial Development of Cincinnati to the Year 1860. Chicago: University of Chicago Libraries, 1938.

King, Willford I. The Wealth and Income of the People of the United
   States. New York: The Macmillan Co., 1915.

La Follette, R.M., Ed. The Making of America. Chicago: The Making
   of America Company, 1906.

Land, J.E. Chicago: the Future Metropolis of the New World.
   Chicago, 1883.

Larson, Henrietta M. Guide to Business History. Cambridge: Harvard
   University Press, 1948.

Lionberger, I.H. The Annals of St. Louis. St. Louis: Missouri
   Historical Society, 1929.

Maher, William H. On the Road to Riches. Toledo: T. Brown, Fager &
   Company, 1876.

Martin, E.W. History of the Grange Movement. Philadelphia:
   National Publishing Company, 1873.

McCormick Co. Pioneering with Products and People. Baltimore:
   McCormick and Company, 1939.

McLaughlin, Glenn E. Growth of American Manufacturing Areas.
   Pittsburgh: University of Pittsburgh Bureau of Business
   Research, 1938.

Meagher, T.F. The Commercial Agency System of the United States and
   Canada Exposed. New York, 1876.

Miller, W.H. History of Kansas City. Kansas City: Birdsall &
   Miller, 1881.

Moody, W.D. Men Who Sell Things. Chicago: A.C. McClerg Co., 1908.

Morley, L.H., Powell, S.H. 1600 Business Books. New York: H.W.
   Wilson Co., 1917.

Morrison, Andrew. The Industries of Cincinnati. Cincinnati:
   Metropolitan Publishing Co., 1886.

Moses, J., and Kirkland, J., ed. The History of Chicago, Illinois.
   Chicago: Nunsell and Co., 1895. 2 vols.

National Food Brokers Association. Food Brokers. Washington, 1945.

National Wholesale Conference, Report of Committee I. Wholesalers'
Functions and Services. Washington: Chamber of Commerce of the
United States, 1929.

National Wholesale Conference, Report of Committee II. Economic
Factors Affecting Wholesaling. Washington: Chamber of Commerce
of the United States, 1929.

Nisbet, H.T. Footprints on the Road. New York: Martin Brown Co.,
1903.

Norvell, Saunders. Forty Years of Hardware. New York: Hardware
Age, 1924.

Nourse, Edwin G. The Chicago Produce Market. Boston: Houghton
Mifflin Company, 1918.

One Hundred Years Progress of the United States. Hartford, Conn:
L. Stebbins, 1872.

Parkins, A.E. The South: Its Economic-Geographic Development. New
York: J. Wiley and Sons, 1938.

Pennsylvania Historical Review. City of Philadelphia. New York,
1886.

Presbrey, Frank. The History and Development of Advertising. New
York: Doubleday, Doran and Co., 1929.

Rowell, George R. Forty Years an Advertising Agent. New York:
Printers' Ink Publishing Company, 1905.

Savay, Norbert. Principles of Foreign Trade. New York: Ronald
Press Co., 1919.

Scharf, J.T., and Wescott, T. History of Philadelphia.
Philadelphia: L.H. Ewerts and Co., 1884, Vol. III.

Semple, E. and Jones. History and Its Geographic Conditions.
Boston: Houghton Mifflin Company, 1933.

Shirk, A. Urban. Marketing Through Food Brokers. New York: McGraw-
Hill Company, Inc., 1939.

Shutter, M.D. History of Minneapolis. Chicago: S.J. Clarke
Publishing Co., 1922.

Smith, William. *Annual Statement of the Trade and Commerce of Cincinnati for Commercial Year Ending August 3, 1859.* Cincinnati, 1859.

Sprague, J.R. *The Middleman.* New York: William Morrow & Co., 1928.

Stevens, W.B. *St. Louis the Fourth City, 1764-1911.* St. Louis: S.J. Clarke Publishing Co., 1911.

Stoddard, W.O. *Men of Business.* New York: Putnam, 1893.

Subcommittee on Memorial History Boston Tercentenary Committee. *Fifty Years of Boston 1880-1930.* Boston, 1932.

Thorp, W., and Mitchell, W. *Business Annals, 1790-1925.* New York: National Bureau of Economic Research, 1926.

Wright, John S. *Chicago: Past Present and Future.* Chicago: Horton and Leonard, 1868.

Wright, John S. *Chicago, Relations to the Great Interior.* Chicago: Horton and Leonard, 1870.

Wright, Richardson. *Hawkers and Walkers in Early America.* Philadelphia: J.B. Lippincott Co., 1927.

Articles

Berry, T.S. "Wholesale Commodity Prices in the Ohio Valley, 1816-1860," *Review of Economic Statistics*, August, 1935.

Bigelow, Samuel A. "Fifty Years in the Hardware Business," *Iron Age*, January 4, 1906, p. 150.

"Cone Mills: Old King Denim," *Fortune*, January, 1953, p. 87.

Copeland, Melvin T. "Managerial Factor in Marketing," *Facts and Factors in Economic History*. Cambridge: Harvard University Press, 1932, p. 596.

Dudley, R.M. "The Hardware Trade of the South," *Iron Age*, January 4, 1906, p. 154.

Engle, N.H. "An Estimate of the Volume of Wholesale Trade in the United States, 1899-1935," *Survey of Current Business*, May, 1936, p. 16.

Eableman, B.F. "The South Fifty Years Ago," Iron Age, January 4, 1906, p. 166.

Fernley, T.J. "The National Hardware Association," Iron Age, January 4, 1906, p. 157.

Gage, R.W. "The Mix-Up Centering Around the Jobber," Printers' Ink, August 11, 1910, p. 8.

"Glossary of Commercial Terms," The Banker's Magazine, January, 1861, p. 545.

Gras, N.S.B. "The Rise of Big Business," Journal of Economic and Business History, May, 1932, p. 381.

Hall, A.N. "The Old Wholesale Peddler and his Teams," New England Magazine, Vol. 28, 1900, p. 690.

"How the Jobber Pulled the House Down on Himself," Printers' Ink, August 25, 1910, p. 38.

Jones, Edward J. "The Manufacturer and the Domestic Market," Annals of the American Academy of Political and Social Science, January, 1905, p. 1.

Jones, Owen T. "Factoring," Harvard Business Review, Winter, 1936, p. 186.

Journal of Marketing, Vol. XIV, September, 1949, Special Wholesale Supplement.

Kinley, David. "Credit Instruments in Business Transactions," Journal of Political Economy, March, 1897, p. 157.

Marburg, T.F. "Manufacturer's Drummer, 1852," Bulletin of the Business Historical Society, Vol. XXII: 3, June, 1948.

McCann, A.W. "Looking Back upon the U.S. without a Jobber in 1925," Printers' Ink, July 28, 1910, p. 56.

Page, E.D. "Lessons of the Claflin Crash," The Independent, July 13, 1914.

Philadelphia Board of Trade. "The Distributing and Jobbing Trade of Philadelphia," Twenty-Seventh Annual Report of the Philadelphia Board of Trade, Philadelphia, 1860.

257

Ritter, J.H. "Present Day Jobbing," Annals of the American Academy of Political and Social Science, 1903, p. 451.

Saxton, A.H. "Jobbing Trade Fifty Years Ago," Iron Age, January 4, 1906, p. 148.

Shaw, A.W. "Some Problems in Market Distribution," Quarterly Journal of Economics, August, 1912, p. 703.

Sheldon, O.W. "Old Shipping Merchants of New York," Harper's Monthly, February, 1892, p. 457.

Simmons, E.C. "A Half Century of Hardware," Iron Age, January 4, 1906, p. 145.

Skinner, Edward M. "Credits and Collections in a Wholesale House," The Businessman's Library. Chicago: The System Company, 1907, p. 85.

Smith, R.A. "The Ninety-Nine Lives of Charlie Soames," Fortune, January, 1953, p. 100.

Stone, A.H. "Cotton Factorage System of the Southern States," The American Historical Review, April, 1915, p. 557.

Thompson, C.W. "Relations of Jobbers and Commission Men to the Handling of Produce," Annals of the American Academy of Political and Social Sciences, November, 1913, p. 57.

Ukers, William H. "The Romance of Package Coffee," Nation's Business, July, 1923, p. 40.

Urner, Frank G. "Wholesale City Distribution of Farm Products," Annals of the American Academy of Political and Social Sciences, November, 1913, p. 69.

Weld, L.D.H. "Marketing Agencies Between Manufacturers and Jobbers," Quarterly Journal of Economics, August, 1917, p. 571.

Westerfield, Roy B. "Early History of American Auctions--A Chapter in Commercial History," Connecticut Academy of Arts and Sciences, May, 1920, p. 159.

Government Publications

Annual Reports of the Comptroller of the State of New York. Albany, 1861-1894.

Boston Laws and Ordinances, 1864.

Charter and Ordinances of Chicago. September 15, 1856.

City of St. Louis Ordinances, 1856.

Documents of the Assembly of the State of New York, No. 64. Albany, 1878.

Documents of the Assembly of the State of New York, No. 218. Albany, 1849.

Federal Trade Commission. Chain Store Inquiry. Washington: Government Printing Office, 1932-35.

Industrial Commission. Distribution of Farm Products, Vol. VI. Washington: Government Printing Office, 1901.

Industrial Commission. Final Report of the Industrial Commission, Vol. XIX. Washington: Government Printing Office, 1902.

Industrial Commission. Labor, Manufactures and General Business, Vol. VII. Washington: Government Printing Office, 1900.

Industrial Commission. Trusts and Industrial Combinations, Vol. I, XIII. Washington: Government Printing Office, 1900.

New York State Laws Relating to the City of New York, 1862.

Report of the National Conservation Commission. Washington: Government Printing Office, 1909.

Report of the Special Commissioner of the Revenue. House Executive Documents No. 81, 40th Congress, 2nd Session, January 7, 1868.

Senate Documents, 72nd Congress, 1st Session. Chain Stores. Washington: Government Printing Office, 1932.

Treasury Department, Bureau of Statistics. Reports on the Internal Commerce of the United States. (1876, 1880, 1887, 1890).

U.S. Census, 1900: Occupations at the Twelfth Census.

United States Department of Commerce. Effective Use of Wholesale Drug Warehouses. Washington: Government Printing Office, 1947.

United States Department of Commerce, Bureau of the Census. *Historical Statistics of the United States*, 1789-1945. Washington: Government Printing Office, 1949.

United States Department of Commerce. *Modernizing and Operating Grocery Warehouses*. Washington: Government Printing Office, 1951.

U.S. House of Representatives, *Report of the Comission upon the Best Methods of Securing More Intimate International and Commercial Relations Between the U.S. and Central America and South America*. Washington: Government Printing Office, 1885.

Wholesale Prices, Wages, and Transportation. Senate Report #1894, 2nd Session 52nd Congress.

Periodicals

Bulletin of the Business Historical Society.

Commercial and Financial Chronicle. New York, 1865–

De Bow's Review. New Orleans, 1847–69.

Hunt's Merchant and Commercial Review. New York, 1839–70.

University Studies

Atherton, Lewis E. "The Pioneer Merchant in Mid-America," *University of Missouri Studies*, Volume XIV, No. 2, April, 1939.

Hartsborough, M.L. "The Twin Cities as a Metropolitan Market," *University of Minnesota Studies in the Social Sciences*, Number 18, 1925.

Hutchinson, W.G. "Decentralization in Grocery Jobbing," *Kansas Studies in Business*, No. 5, Lawrence, 1926.

Jones, Fred M. "Middlemen in the Domestic Trade of the United States," *Illinois Studies in the Social Sciences*. Volume 21, No. 3, 1937.

University of Illinois, Bureau of Business Research. *Grocery Wholesaling in Illinois*, 1900-1929. Bulletin No. 36, Urbana, 1931.

For Product Safety Concerns and Information please contact our EU
representative GPSR@taylorandfrancis.com Taylor & Francis Verlag GmbH,
Kaufingerstraße 24, 80331 München, Germany

Printed and bound by CPI Group (UK) Ltd, Croydon, CR0 4YY

01/05/2025

01858451-0001